PRAISE FOR *HI* *HIGH-TOUCH RE*

"Barbara Bruno is the rare individual who can cover strategy and immediate tactics to ensure success in a single book. It doesn't matter if you are an experienced recruiter or just starting on the journey with recruiting as a career, I have not encountered a more engaging person than Barbara. She instantly connects with her audience and provides immediate value, not just theory, to help you achieve success!"
Randy Marmon, CEO, Lucas Group

"In this book, Barbara Bruno unravels the ways in which ever-changing technological advances affect communication—and consequently recruiting and talent acquisition—and how to utilize tech, in conjunction with the human touch, to enhance the candidate experience. The tools and techniques Bruno outlines are particularly engaging, as they draw on her vast experience within the industry. Featuring immersive and actionable subject matter, and comprehensive online resources, this book is a significant contribution to the recruiting profession."
Tammi Heaton, Chief Operating Officer, PrideStaff

"Barbara Bruno is an outstanding trainer, speaker, and, most importantly, listener. Her experience as an advisor to scores of recruiters has been distilled in this comprehensive look at sound competitive strategies. This should be a go-to for recruiters looking to hone their skills for success."
Ron Herzon, CEO, Fortune Franchise Corporation

"We have benefitted from Barbara Bruno's insights over the past few years, and now everyone else has the same opportunity to learn from her. The insights she provides is the differentiation from being a recruiter to a workforce workplace expert. This is a must-read for anyone working in the

recruiting or staffing profession. This should be utilized as a reference guide and not a one-time read with all the golden nuggets of information Barbara has provided, as our profession embraces the need for a high-tech but also a high-touch approach."
Pat Patel, CEO, Intelliswift Software, Inc.

"For the past 18 years, I've been a student of Barbara Bruno's philosophies, training and education. Barbara continues to raise the bar with her newest book and I encourage any recruiting professional who wants to amplify their career to take the time and read her latest achievement."
Robert Krzak, President, Gecko Hospitality

"We have had the distinct pleasure of knowing and working with Barbara Bruno for several years. Her contributions to our company, bolstered by her vast experience, have been immeasurable. This book is a gold mine and veritable roadmap on how to succeed on every level in staffing. Whether you are an owner, manager, account manager or recruiter, this book will give you the shortcut to the greatest staffing techniques known to the industry. This book will be required reading for all of our employees going forward!"
Eric F. Brady, CEO, and Richard J. Mainz, CFO, Mainz Brady Group

"A comprehensive, thorough primer that offers a firm foundation for a newbie and a superlative review for a pro. If recruiting is something you feel you might excel at or if you have already experienced the passion of one of the most fulfilling professions, this is required reading. This book is one of a kind, written by the leading trainer to the staffing and recruiting professions."
Kenneth J. Bohan, President/CEO, The Liberty Group

"Barbara Bruno is always on point, direct, and provides relevant content. Anyone reading this book will obtain information they can immediately put into action to improve their success in the recruiting profession. This book proves the relevance of a high-tech high-touch approach while continuing to improve the candidate experience. I love Barbara's 'say it like it is' style and would highly recommend this book."
Jeri Meyers, EVP of Sales, QPS Employment Group

"Barbara proves with great alacrity and insight how technological advance, when paralleled with the art of communication through high-touch resource, is crucial to all business growth and ongoing success."
Johanne Berry, CPC, C.M. Presidente, Strategie et Rayonnement d'affaire, Gestion Johanne Berry, Inc.

"Barbara Bruno is the go-to expert in the professional field of recruiting and this book is a must-read. Her passion and commitment to help recruiters attain success and provide a positive experience for the candidates we represent is apparent in every chapter. Even the most experienced recruiters will benefit from the comprehensive materials in this book."
Robert Maltzman, Vice President, Sales, SMCI Software Management Consultants, Inc.

High-Tech High-Touch Recruiting

How to attract and retain the best talent by improving the candidate experience

Barbara Bruno

KoganPage

Publisher's note

Every possible effort has been made to ensure that the information contained in this book is accurate at the time of going to press, and the publishers and authors cannot accept responsibility for any errors or omissions, however caused. No responsibility for loss or damage occasioned to any person acting, or refraining from action, as a result of the material in this publication can be accepted by the editor, the publisher or the author.

First published in Great Britain and the United States in 2021 by Kogan Page Limited

2nd Floor, 45 Gee Street	122 W 27th St, 10th Floor	4737/23 Ansari Road
London	New York, NY 10001	Daryaganj
EC1V 3RS	USA	New Delhi 110002
United Kingdom		India
www.koganpage.com		

Kogan Page books are printed on paper from sustainable forests.

ISBNs

Hardback	978 1 78966 517 8
Paperback	978 1 78966 515 4
Ebook	978 1 78966 516 1

Library of Congress Control Number

2020941952

British Library Cataloguing-in-Publication Data

A CIP record for this book is available from the British Library.

Typeset by Integra Software Services, Pondicherry
Print production managed by Jellyfish
Printed and bound by CPI Group (UK) Ltd, Croydon CR0 4YY

CONTENTS

Online resources for this book can be found at
https://koganpage.box.com/v/HighTechHighTouchResources.

ABOUT THE AUTHOR

Barbara Bruno is an internationally recognized recruiting expert who has a proven track record of helping recruiters and talent acquisition professionals become more successful and less stressed. Driven by her passion for the recruiting profession, she takes pride in the thousands of candidates her firm has placed in jobs and the strong relationships she establishes with hiring authorities.

In addition to speaking at more than 25 conferences annually, she has created online tutorials distributed globally that provide comprehensive recruiting and sales training. She was instrumental in helping launch a certification program for the recruiting profession, by writing a study guide of best practices.

She has been recognized by many associations for her leadership, volunteerism, and extraordinary commitment to improve and promote the recruiting profession. To improve the overall candidate experience, she also created an innovative career portal, so companies can now help 100 percent of the candidates they attract.

Barbara has been married to her husband, Tony, for 32 years, has five children and eleven grandchildren, and resides in Merrillville, Indiana. She spends her spare time with her family, painting, baking, and playing piano. Her website is www.goodasgoldtraining.com.

Introduction

In grammar school, I was encouraged by my teachers to write stories or poems because I talked too much in class. Who could have predicted that talking too much and my love of writing would lead me to the recruiting profession, teaching and training other recruiters, and writing this book?

One of the best decisions I made many years ago was to enter the recruiting profession. I had become a single parent and knew sales was the only profession that offered unlimited earning potential. Up until then, I had been employed as a real estate broker, but with interest rates over 20 percent, homes were not selling. I decided to pursue a different sales career and had heard that employment agencies had access to jobs not advertised. It was a different time, and women were seen in four primary roles: secretary, nurse, teacher, or homemaker. It didn't help that I typed over 100 words per minute due to my piano training. As a result, I was asked by every recruiter "How fast can you type?" even though I was seeking a sales position.

I can remember how defeated I felt when I was told I had no sales ability and was destined to be a secretary. I knew I could not support my daughters on a secretarial salary and knew my ex-husband would provide no financial support. I was 28 years old and scared to death but decided to double-mortgage my home and open an employment agency. I vowed to treat everyone the way I would want to be treated, listen to understand their priorities, and treat them with respect. I also vowed I would never limit career opportunities for women to four traditional roles and worked especially hard helping single moms who found themselves in a similar situation to mine. In fact, the first three employees I hired were moms who were the sole supporters of their families.

The name of my first company was Sunshine Employment because I wanted to put "sunshine into the lives of the people I represented."

My competition were all men, and most of them had tested my typing and told me I couldn't sell. I had proven I could sell in the real estate profession, and rather than let others' opinions define me, I adopted the attitude of "just watch me." However, even though I was working long hours and putting my best efforts into my new business, I almost proved them right. I struggled for almost a year and finally realized recruiting was much different than real estate. I needed training, or I might lose my business.

I opened my business pre-internet or YouTube, and the information that I could find in books provided an overview of recruiting but didn't teach how to establish a successful recruiting firm. I reached out to other business owners in the recruiting profession, but no one was willing to mentor me. Out of desperation, I called the National Association of Personnel Services (NAPS) and asked if they provided training. They shared details of their annual conference that would be held in the fall, but I didn't know if I would still be in business by fall. Realizing I needed training before their conference, they suggested I attend a one-day training event in Chicago presented by a well-known trainer in the recruiting profession, Tony Bruno. Throughout the day of training, I realized there were recruiting and client development processes that I needed to learn. I invested in Tony's training manual and tapes, which also included scripts and forms. Hearing him in person and most importantly implementing the processes he taught turned my company around.

I made a commitment to a lifetime of learning and attended the NAPS conference every year. Ironically, years later I served on the board of directors and became the chair of the board of NAPS. I was also contracted by TechServe Alliance to create a certification program of best practices for recruiters and account executives who place IT, engineering and accounting professionals, and contractors. I speak at NAPS and TSA every year and value my affiliations with these associations.

To me, recruiting is so much more than merely a profession. Recruiting is a calling that appeals to people who are passionate about having a positive impact on the lives of others. I found it very rewarding to help companies achieve their goals and objectives by providing them with the best talent. At the same time, I helped the candidates I represented advance their careers, which not only impacted my candidates but also the people they loved. It's extremely fulfilling to improve the quality of my life by helping others improve theirs. It became obvious early in my career that next to good health, money has the greatest impact on a person's life. Each time I helped negotiate a higher compensation package for one of my candidates, I knew it improved the quality of their life and provided them with more options. When you have money, you have choices; when you don't, your choices are limited.

I was once contacted by the Texas Association of Personnel Consultants to train in various cities. A few days before I flew to Texas a hurricane hit Houston, so instead of going to Houston first, I would fly there last. When I was driving from the airport to my hotel, I saw hundreds of people who had lost their homes sleeping outside. When I arrived at the Hyatt Hotel, there were also many families in the lobby waiting for a room. It hit me that the people who had money were waiting for a hotel room, while those who didn't were sleeping outside and had limited options. This experience made me more committed than ever to my profession. I knew I was helping people improve their incomes and live the life they deserved to live. I wanted the candidates I represented to have more options when faced with life's issues.

When I travel for work, I'm often asked what I do for a living. My response is always the same: "I change lives for the better." From my response, many people assume I am employed in one of the typical helping professions, such as teaching, social work, or coaching. While most people wouldn't consider recruiting a helping profession, I think it is. In working with clients and candidates, I find myself teaching hiring authorities how to conduct a job interview, providing career advice and coaching to candidates, and even counseling clients or candidates who have run into obstacles in their search for the perfect candidate or job opportunity. I also learned how important it was to fine-tune my listening skills. Technology has dramatically changed the way people communicate, with many people choosing a text over a conversation. When I position myself as the best listener in the lives of my clients and candidates, I do a better job for them and create lifetime relationships that benefit them, as well as myself.

In my 30 years as a recruiter, I've made many mistakes. Many of those mistakes were avoidable, costly, and often limited my success. In retrospect, I see those mistakes as valuable moments of learning but don't want others in the recruiting profession to make the same mistakes. (Later in my career, I realized it's much smarter and less costly to learn from the mistakes of others!)

I wrote this book to share what I have learned throughout my career so I can help those in the recruiting or talent acquisition professions avoid pitfalls and successfully fill more requisitions with the best talent. If you're new to the recruiting profession, my hope is that this book will help you avoid some of the lessons that I learned the hard way. If you're an experienced recruiter, my hope is that this book will provide you with additional tools and techniques that can help you be more successful. If there's one thing I know for sure, things will continue to change due to technology. That is why I've personally made a lifetime commitment to learning and trying new techniques, so I can help others achieve an even greater level of success.

Like me, I'm sure you seek to keep updated on our profession by reading books about recruiting, taking online courses, or attending conferences. In preparing to write this book, I reviewed many books, articles, and courses. While there is an abundance of information about recruiting online, in books, and through other resources, I find myself often cringing at some of the content. In one article I read, the author was advising recruiters to establish "candidate and hiring authority control." Can you remember what happened the last time someone tried to control you? Or, if you're a parent, have you ever tried to control your children? The results are usually not positive. I believe we have a responsibility as recruiters to establish rapport based on trust, and trust is something you must earn by your actions. It's about consistently doing your job ethically and responsibly and being a true advocate for the candidates you represent.

I was also surprised at how few sources address the potentially negative impact, as well as the benefits, of technology on our profession. When I entered this profession, there were no applicant tracking systems, customer relationship management systems, or social media platforms like Facebook, Twitter, or LinkedIn. There were also relatively few job boards, so all applicant searching was done by running classified ads, referrals, or cold calling. At that time, recruiting was primarily a high-touch relationship-building process. As the years went by, I witnessed recruiting become less and less high touch and more and more high tech.

While I believe the various types of technology we use in recruiting are extremely helpful, I am discouraged by the many clients and candidates who hide behind technology, using texting, voicemail, and email when a phone call or an in-person meeting would be more effective. Recruiting technologies can enhance efficiency, but they don't replace the importance of high-touch relationship building. After all, computers don't fill requisitions—people do! When a hiring process is too automated, very qualified candidates can be screened out by automated systems screening for keywords. The human touch and input are critical in the hiring process, if your goal is to present the best talent who not only get hired but will become engaged and retained employees.

How this book is organized

In a candidate-driven market, time is of the essence. In Chapter 1, I address how a company's hiring process can either help or hurt their recruiting efforts. I outline suggestions how recruiters can play a key role in helping update the five aspects of the hiring process where many companies waste the most time and energy—job requisitions, hiring parameters, performance objectives, the interview process, and candidate appraisal. I realize you may not be able to personally implement the changes, but if you position yourself as a workforce/workplace expert to individuals involved in the hiring process, you can encourage others to initiate change that will improve the hiring process.

Recruiters can present the best candidates who are the perfect fit for an opportunity, but if companies have an outdated or inefficient hiring process, those delays could result in losing the perfect candidate. The best candidates know they are in demand and need only reach out to their network to identify other competing job opportunities.

An updated hiring process that is lean and efficient can help your hiring managers interview and hire the best talent. If you're a third-party recruiter, you have the added challenge of working with many clients who each have a specific hiring process. Position yourself as a workforce/workplace expert who can share facts to prove how their hiring process is hindering their efforts to attract top talent. When they experience improved results, you elevate the relationship you have with your clients.

Hiring authorities expect us to identify the best talent, not just candidates in an active job search who normally only represent about 15 percent of the global talent pool. In Chapter 2, I address how to effectively identify and communicate with the best talent. I'm always surprised to find out that many recruiters have resorted to "posting and praying" versus proactively recruiting top talent. When I'm training recruiters, I always hear the same complaint—candidates are hard to find. A candidate-driven market is very good for individuals in the recruiting profession. In fact, there has never been a better time in history to be a recruiter because of the global shortage of top talent. If it were simple to hire top talent, your services would not be needed. However, you can't only represent candidates who are answering website postings or job board ads. You must recruit the best talent who are often currently working (these are called passive candidates) but would consider a new opportunity if it represents their next career move. In fact, when I'm speaking to audiences of hiring authorities, I'm often asked "When did recruiters stop recruiting?" It's the recruited passive candidates whom hiring authorities prefer to hire.

In Chapter 2, I help you learn how to identify high performers, where to find them using high-tech and high-touch methods, and how to communicate with them in order to pique their interest to consider other opportunities. If you are currently just texting or emailing candidates because you believe they don't want to talk with you, this chapter is for you. I reveal how to communicate with prospective candidates so that they realize the benefit of talking to you. Part of being a good communicator is knowing when and how to listen. Listening enables you to hear what is most important to your candidate and ask the questions that will reveal their long-term goals and motivations. Having this information will enable you to advocate for them during your recruiting efforts.

If you haven't recruited passive candidates before, I share some sample scripts for your initial conversation as well as a few scripts on how to overcome candidate objections. Early in my career, I hung up when I heard objections because I viewed them as obstacles. Later in my career, I learned objections were a request for more information or a buying sign. In order to recruit the most qualified candidates, you must be great at overcoming objections. I also provide some guidance for how you can effectively overcome the most common candidate objections.

Chapter 3 will teach you how to interview to hire or place the best possible talent. To interview well, you need to understand what information you are looking for so that you can ask the best questions. In this chapter, I outline five key objectives of interviews so that you can create structured interview questions that will surface the information that will enable you to make the best hiring decision. You first need to understand the reason why the position is available, which means finding out what problem the hiring authority is looking to solve by filling this position.

You also need to learn what is most important to the candidates you represent and if they would be a good fit for the opportunity, hiring authority, and company culture. You will also learn to eliminate emotion and bias from your interview process. I've observed recruiters screening in a candidate who was like them and screening out candidates who were not, without realizing they had any bias. Whether they screened a candidate in or out, they could justify their decision. I've also seen candidates who were phenomenal interviewers but failed miserably once hired. Let's face it, interviews are not comfortable for most people unless they have sales experience or are job-hoppers with lots of interviewing experience. Those are not necessarily the best candidates to fill your requisitions.

Throughout my entire career, I've consistently changed the way I interview to align with changes in the job market and talent pool. I outline a structured four-round interview process to help you evaluate and compare candidates quickly and fairly. Instead of simply focusing on skills, experience, and stability, I show you an effective process to accurately identify soft and transferrable skills.

Chapter 4 focuses on the importance of time and timing in the recruiting process. I learned early in my career that recruiting is all about timing-timing-timing. It didn't take me long to realize that we have people on both sides of our process who often change their minds, priorities, and time frame. I have had candidates call me on Sunday night and tell me they decided the timing wasn't right for them to start their job the next day. I'm not sure whether it was harder knowing my candidates decided not to accept the job or sharing this disappointing news with my hiring authority.

As technology has allowed us to find candidates faster, hiring authorities have increased their expectations and expect us to find the best talent faster than at any other time in history. I reveal how to balance the challenge of aligning your candidate's timing with that of your hiring authority. This chapter will also help you anticipate other timing obstacles that can slow down your recruiting process, such as being a few months from becoming vested in a pension fund, waiting periods to become eligible for benefits, higher costs for benefits, vacation time planned, or projects that need to be completed before your candidate can leave their current job.

In Chapter 5, I teach you how to extend offers that will be accepted. A job offer for a new position is so much more than a starting salary and start date. You are asking a candidate to trust you, to take a risk on a new position with a new company. Further, you are asking them to stop pursuing other possible job opportunities. In this chapter, I help you understand and overcome the challenges that you will confront from competitors looking to hire your candidate, from the candidates themselves, and from the hiring authority. You will learn how to prevent offers from being declined along with key strategies to eliminate declined offers.

Throughout my career, I've realized the importance of creating a formal offer letter, tracking metrics, and providing candidates with resignation assistance. I provide a sample offer letter as well as a sample resignation letter that you can use to help you extend job offers that will be accepted. You will also learn how to confirm that your candidates have in fact handed in their two-week notice to their current employer.

In Chapter 6, I help you eliminate surprises and obstacles that can limit your success. I don't know about you, but I loved surprises before I was in the recruiting profession. Unfortunately, surprises in recruiting are usually not in our favor, which is why it's important to proactively anticipate issues.

I can vividly remember a candidate who was the perfect fit for a vice president of human resources position in Chicago. She accepted the job, sold her home, and registered her daughters in a charter school. When the moving van arrived, she told them she had changed her mind overnight and decided not to move to Chicago. She did mention to me during her interview that she had always wanted to start her own business, but as a single mom, she didn't feel she could take the risk. I obviously did not ask probing questions, or I would have known she was serious about becoming an entrepreneur. The hiring authority I was working with was extremely upset that I didn't know she would not be accepting the position. That was the day I made a commitment to listen better, address red flags head on, and never fall victim to "selective hearing." I hope you can learn from my mistake so you don't have a similar experience.

Surprises can be minimized by pre-closing, preparing, and debriefing both your candidates and hiring authorities as well as checking references. Technology will help you locate information quickly, but it's your ability to accurately pre-close, prep, and debrief your candidates and hiring authorities that will prevent you from being blindsided.

The candidate experience is more important than ever in this candidate-driven job market. Unhappy or dissatisfied candidates can reach hundreds or thousands of people in minutes on social media, which affects your ability to recruit the best talent. Paying attention to your candidates' goals and motivations goes a long way toward creating trust and rapport. Most recruiters don't do a good job of following up and nurturing candidates after they are hired or placed, which is the primary reason they don't receive referrals to other qualified candidates. In Chapter 7, I teach you how to nurture candidates and how this helps you receive more referrals of top talent. I conduct a weekly job-seeker call for thousands of job seekers, and I always open the lines for their questions. Their questions have proven to me that most candidates feel we only care about our hiring authorities. If you place someone in a job and they never hear from you again, this perception is validated.

Because there is so much that can go wrong after candidates have handed in their two-week notice, it is important for recruiters to stay in close contact and do what they can to help nurture their candidates through their first day of employment. When starting a new role, candidates are leaving their comfort zone and embarking on a journey to the unknown. You can help them by appointing a mentor, establishing regular communications with them, and answering any questions they have after starting their new role.

We helped an HR generalist advance her career when she accepted a job as a director of HR with a Fortune 500 company. The new job represented increased responsibility and income, and most importantly, the company viewed HR as a strategic partner who could help them improve engagement and retention of talent hired. After just 45 days, during a follow-up conversation with our candidate, she asked us to find her another job because she was doing less than she had done in her generalist position at her last employer. When we reached out to the vice president of HR, she shared her recent diagnosis of cancer and admitted she was giving our candidate busywork as she focused on her health issues. We suggested that she lean on our candidate to lessen her workload and stress. Within three months, she was on medical leave, and our candidate assumed many of the responsibilities of her supervisor. In less than one year, our candidate was promoted to the vice president of HR and was grateful we had stepped in to resolve her initial frustrations. Your nurturing is critical if you want the candidates you recruit to become engaged and retained.

Nurturing your candidates will also provide you with other benefits. By nurturing your candidates and staying in touch with them, they are more likely to refer other qualified candidates to you. The reality is, if candidates you place in jobs aren't referring candidates to you, those candidates are being recruited by your competition. At least 40 percent of the talent you represent should be referred. You will learn how to make that happen and how you benefit by obtaining referrals from your new hires. In addition, hiring authorities who are happy with their engaged employees are likely to hire you to fill other job requisitions.

Chapter 8 is focused on developing the mindset and skills necessary to be successful. As a recruiter, you will inevitably face challenges, delays, and frustrations that can make it hard for you to stay motivated and achieve balance. In my career, I have trained and managed thousands of recruiters and have found that the most successful maintain a positive attitude and mindset even during the most challenging times. It's not the recruiter who works the longest hours who succeeds, but the recruiter who has the right attitude and can learn from their mistakes. With a positive attitude, you can view challenges as opportunities to learn, handle difficult hiring authorities and candidates, and keep yourself focused on what is important so that you can better manage your time. Being focused also helps you hold yourself accountable. I show you the key metric that helps you define your success as a recruiter and hold yourself accountable and the importance of embracing change, which is a constant in this wonderful profession.

This book comes with online resources including sample offer letters, recruiting scripts, job requisitions, an interview scorecard, a listing of characteristics of best hires, and guidelines for a nine-step telephone interview process.

I'm hoping this book inspires you to make a lifetime commitment to the recruiting profession and that you spend your life also changing people's lives for the better. Share your passion about recruiting with me by connecting with me on LinkedIn. I'd love to hear your success story!

Start with updating the hiring process 1

The recruiting profession is experiencing a boom. Worldwide, an estimated $200 billion is spent by companies looking to attract and retain the best talent.[1] The demand for talent is expected to increase as more companies compete for those highly skilled employees who have both technical and soft skills. As a recruiter, your expertise in helping companies attract and retain top talent has never been more valuable.

Yet recruiting is just one step in the hiring process. As a 30-year veteran whose recruiting firm has placed thousands of candidates, I can tell you that it takes more than a talented recruiter to attract the best talent who end up as engaged and retained employees. I've witnessed companies spending thousands of dollars on recruiters and sophisticated recruiting technologies only to end up losing top talent because the candidates get frustrated by excessively long application processes or too many rounds of interviews.

In order to ensure that your company's or client's hiring process is helping and not hurting your recruiting efforts, advise them to regularly evaluate and update their hiring process using a high-tech high-touch approach. You can use the most current high-tech software in order to find qualified candidates more quickly, but you also need human interaction to create a hiring process that attracts the talent needed to achieve company goals, assists the recruiter in attracting candidates, aligns job requirements with internal stakeholder needs, and ensures that candidates have a positive experience.

Consider your current hiring process or, if you're a third-party recruiter, the hiring processes utilized by each of your clients, and ask yourself the following questions: Have you lost top talent because of an overly complicated interview process? Have you brought in qualified candidates only to find out that you were recruiting based on an outdated job requisition? Do you struggle to get agreement with hiring managers on performance objectives? Do all hiring managers use the same criteria to evaluate candidates? How much time is spent at each stage of the process, from identifying the hiring need to extending the job offer? Review the questions that you answered yes and realize those are the areas of the hiring process that could be sabotaging your ability to fill open requisitions. Ask these questions of the individuals who can approve these changes to improve their current hiring process. If you focus on how implementing the changes will benefit them or how they are losing talent or money, you will expedite the time it takes to initiate changes in the hiring process.

Throughout my career in recruiting, I've observed that companies waste the most time and energy and money on five aspects of the hiring process:

1 Job requisitions

The job requisition is the roadmap for the recruiting process. Unfortunately, that roadmap is often outdated, boring, and repetitive. Most requisitions are simply a list of required skills, credentials, experience, and education.

2 Hiring parameters

Many companies have outdated flextime, work-from-home, or compensation practices that may be hurting their recruiting efforts.

3 Performance objectives

When you determine performance objectives up front, everyone involved in the hiring process knows exactly what is expected of a new hire, which saves time not only during the interview process, but when it comes to choosing a qualified candidate.

4 Interview process

The most effective interview process should be limited to a four-step process. Limiting your interview cycle to four rounds has been found to reduce a company's average time to hire by almost two weeks, saving employees and candidates hundreds of hours in interview time.[2]

5 Candidate appraisal

When you have multiple individuals involved in appraising a candidate, it's important to create consistency in the appraisal process and ensure that emotion and bias are removed from the decision-making.

Job requisitions

Your job requisition is a type of marketing collateral. Your job requisition needs to identify what the company requires as well as provide candidates with a sense of the company culture and outline opportunities for professional development and growth. Millennials are the largest part of the workforce that you'll be hiring, and they want to know what they will be doing every day, what challenges they will face, what kinds of development they will receive, and how their work will matter. They want to understand how the work they do contributes to the company goals and mission.

Unfortunately, most traditional job requisitions are simply a list of required skills, credentials, experience, and education that are used to screen out candidates instead of screen in top talent. A skills-based job requisition may even put you at a disadvantage when you're recruiting for top talent. Think of it this way. When someone accepts a job, they perform the tasks outlined in their job description. However, as employees grow in their roles, they add value in other ways by using other skills they might have. (Think of some of your past jobs and how your responsibilities grew from your first month of employment to your first year of employment.) Managers appreciate this extra effort at first and, over time, expect that anyone who can do the job well will have these extra skills. Ironically, when a hiring authority uses the additional skills of the current employee, these skills are rarely included in the job requisition because chances are the requisition has not been updated.

However, reducing the position to a list of skills is not going to attract the best talent. And as a recruiter, you have the additional challenge of finding a new person with the exact same skills as the person who preceded them. In addition, if you recruit a candidate who has the specific set of skills and has done the exact same job, they will not see the job as an opportunity for growth—in fact, they may view the job as a lateral move and have concerns that accepting the job could limit their growth. When a candidate is hired based only on a specific set of skills, they often become a costly turnover statistic, because they are not challenged by the work. When the candidates you present don't succeed, this indirectly affects your success as a recruiter.

Retaining employees is not only critical for you as a recruiter, but is critical to the long-term success of the hiring authority. According to the Society for Human Resource Management, "The business ramifications of employee turnover are enormous. Each departure costs approximately one-third of that worker's annual earnings."[3]

To ensure that you are hiring employees who will stay on to become engaged employees, make it a practice to regularly evaluate job requisitions to ensure they speak to the needs of the company as well as the candidate. Focus specifically on the following aspects: job title, performance standards, daily responsibilities, credentials and experience, and company culture, mission, and values.

Establish a job title

In a competitive and constantly changing job market, candidates aren't attracted to confining or standard job titles. Recently, a company asked us to recruit two experienced salespeople and expressed their strong preference to hire women. They further explained that most of their salespeople were men, but their clients were predominantly women. In fact, a new prospect requested that they send a female sales representative, because she had a woman-owned business and preferred to discuss her needs with a woman. This was a request they could not fulfill because the only female on their sales team had recently resigned. After hearing that, I realized their current sales team was 100 percent male. We then discussed possible challenges that can occur when you're the only woman on a sales team. As a result, we set a goal to fill at least two of the three open requisitions with women.

The first thing I discussed with their VP of sales was the job title of "Salesman," which could sabotage their objective to hire women. We discussed the range of roles that fall under the heading of sales, which vary in levels of sophistication, job function, and perception by prospects and clients. Once we reviewed the performance objectives of the job, the title was changed from "Salesman" to "Business Development Manager." They also changed the titles of their current salespeople, which had such a positive impact that they set processes in place to review job titles throughout the entire company. They successfully attracted and hired three experienced female Business Development Managers who consistently hit or surpassed goals set. The title of Business Development Manager is not as creative a title as Master Handshaker, but it was far more effective than Salesman and attracted the right candidates.

If you want to recruit future hires who are creative and outside-the-box thinkers, why should they have an in-the-box job title? Like a compelling brand, a compelling job title is one that promises the fulfillment of an expectation. If you expect your corporate communications department to ensure that your company is in the news, why not let the job titles in that department reflect that and create a position titled "Ambassador of Buzz"[4] as virtual business phone service Grasshopper does? Or if you expect your customer service employees or front desk receptionist to greet all visitors warmly in order to reflect the culture and values of your company, why not create a position called "Director of First Impressions" as publishing firm Houghton Mifflin Harcourt does?[5]

Table 1.1 Creative job titles

Traditional job title	Company	Creative job title
Executive Assistant/Office Manager	Detroit Venture Partners	Catalyst
Homepage Feature Items Manager	eBay	Chief Curator
Progressive Strategist	Ford Motor Co	Head of Global Trends and Futuring

To recruit future hires who are creative and out-of-the-box thinkers, consider providing them with an out-of-the-box job title. See the examples in Table 1.1.

Identify performance standards

Clarifying performance standards ensures that everyone involved in the hiring process—the hiring manager, the recruiter, and the job candidate—understands what is expected and how performance will be judged. Before you begin to create or revise a job requisition, ask the hiring manager one very important question: "How will this person be evaluated at the end of six months or at the end of a year?" Keep this information in the forefront when writing your job requisition.

When you determine performance objectives up front, everyone involved in the hiring process knows exactly what is expected of a new hire, which saves time not only during the interview process, but also when it comes to choosing qualified candidates. And when the successful candidate accepts the position, the performance objectives serve as a guide for the person to achieve success. They are also the foundation for the candidate's annual performance review and compensation increase considerations.

Convey daily responsibilities

Remembering that Millennials are the majority in the workforce, your job requisition needs to accurately describe the day-to-day responsibilities, expectations, and standards of performance of the position and provide a sense of how this role fits within the department, team, and company. It should also be concise enough that prospective candidates need only scan a few bullet points to determine if they are qualified and interested.

Define required credentials and experience

Use your performance standards as a guide to define the credentials and experience required, but be careful not to be too restrictive when screening out candidates. If you find a candidate performing in a similar job but with less experience than you require, you don't want to screen them out—they may be a peak performer. It's important to understand the DNA of peak performers, which include the following: they are promoted faster, obtain raises faster, receive recognition for their achievements, and often handle responsibilities well above their job title or experience level.

Share your company culture, mission, and values

For many prospective hires, company culture, mission, and values are almost as important as compensation. Candidates want to work somewhere where they are comfortable not only with the job, but with the people, mission, and core values. Candidates pick up on aspects of company culture in a variety of ways. For example, a company that offers opportunities for professional development, mentorship, or internal advancement is showing that it is interested in attracting employees who will grow their careers with the company. Similarly, companies that offer on-site fitness facilities, complementary gym memberships, or nutritious snacks or lunches are demonstrating their eagerness to attract and retain employees who seek to live a healthy, balanced life.

As you develop your job requisitions, be sure to communicate aspects of your culture that are attractive to the talent you are seeking. If your office is casual, mention that you have a casual dress code or pet-friendly workplace. If you are a highly virtual organization or if you are competing for scarce talent that may not live close by, be sure to mention your flexible work schedule or work-from-home policy. These insights are critical for conveying company values and should be included as an important element of every job requisition. While they may not be a selling point for every candidate, they will be the selling point for the right candidate who will not only be qualified for your job, but will also flourish within your company culture.

Putting it all together

When updated regularly and written with the needs of both the company and the candidate in mind, your job requisition should serve as a strategic marketing tool that will not only attract the best talent but will save you time in the interview process. The job requisition example in Table 1.2 meets all the criteria for attracting the top talent.

Regularly review and update

Now that you have a model for writing job requisitions, it is important to make sure that they are reviewed and updated regularly. At the end of six months or a year, you'll want to ask yourself the following questions to see if these changes have made your hiring process more effective.

- Has the caliber of candidates attracted to my job postings improved?
- Has the caliber of candidates I'm recruiting improved?
- Am I filling open requisitions faster?
- What percentage of new hires become engaged, productive employees?

Your ability to review and revise will continue to improve your recruiting efforts and your ability to fill a higher percentage of open requisitions.

Table 1.2 Job requisition example

Job title: Talent Partner, Gradient Ventures

COMPANY CULTURE AND MISSION

Our mission is to organize the world's information and make it universally accessible and useful. Our company culture offers true flexibility, the freedom to be creative, a fun environment, a dog-friendly workplace, shared values across the organization, constant innovation, trust, alignment with employees' wants and needs, a growth and improvement mindset, a clear purpose, and dedicated focus on employee happiness.

RESPONSIBILITIES

Google's known for our innovative technologies, products, and services—and for the people behind them. As part of our recruiting team, you're charged with finding the most interesting candidates who bring an entrepreneurial spirit and a diversity of thought to all they do. You're responsible for guiding candidates through our hiring process and connecting them to the magic of working at Google. You are creative and driven, which allows you to develop lasting relationships with both candidates and hiring managers. You're also comfortable with numbers and drawing insights from analytics to make our hiring process smarter and more efficient.

Gradient Ventures is Google's AI-focused seed-stage venture fund. Talent is a key ingredient in a company's success and helping companies get the right team members at the right time is invaluable. As a Talent Partner, you will lead all facets of the talent function at Gradient Ventures. You will bring strategic mindset combined with the insight and rigor of a venture partner alongside the relationship building skills of an executive search partner. You will be key in supporting Gradient decisions and operations internally as well as be the external face for Gradient as a speaker at industry events.

Great just isn't good enough for our People Operations Team (you probably know us better as "Human Resources"). Made up of equal parts HR professionals, former consultants, and analysts, we're the advocates of Google's colorful culture. In People Ops, we "find them, grow them and keep them." We bring in the world's most innovative people to Google and provide the programs that help them thrive. Whether recruiting the next Googler, refining our core programs, developing talent, or simply looking for ways to inject some more fun into the lives of our Googlers, we bring a data-driven approach that is reinventing the human resources field.

PERFORMANCE OBJECTIVES

1. **Assess Talent Needs:** Across Gradient's portfolio companies, understand the specific nuances and culture of each organization and, in collaboration with the entrepreneurs, drive outcomes that change the trajectory of a company.

2. **Create and Lead a Talent Program:** Focus on identifying and forming a strong perspective on the next-gen set of AI entrepreneurs, companies, and executive talent for the Gradient portfolio.

(*continued*)

Table 1.2 (Continued)

---

3. **Set an Executive Talent Strategy:** Leverage your knowledge of HR/Talent, operations and venture capital, and/or private equity space to set and execute talent strategy and influence founders and senior leadership.

4. **Gradient's Operational Strategy:** Help develop and execute Gradient's operational strategy.

5. **Lead Community Engagement:** Lead community engagement initiatives and expansion of Gradient's core team and portfolio companies.

MINIMUM QUALIFICATIONS

- BA/BS degree or equivalent practical experience.
- Nine years of experience in VC/PE, or investment banking with experience.
- Experience as an early employee of a fund, founder of technology startup, or in operations at a startup.
- Experience in talent acquisition, organizational design, business consulting, and/or coaching and development.

PREFERRED QUALIFICATIONS

- STEM degree and/or Master's degree.
- Experience influencing through relationships, expertise and data, and ability to manage stakeholders.
- Product management experience in the technology industry (specifically internet, media, consumer hardware, and/or software).
- Communication and interpersonal skills with a proven ability to take initiative and build productive relationships.
- Ability to identify and galvanize this complex web of relationships and dependencies to holistically solve problems and seize opportunities.
- Analytical and problem-solving skills; ability to analyze data, understand trends, and develop recommendations for action based on the analysis.

Hiring parameters

Hiring parameters are those aspects of the role that are aligned with company policy and are essentially nonnegotiables. Some examples of hiring parameters include established working hours (is it a 12-hour workday or an 8-hour workday?), where the office is located and whether the company offers compensation for gas or public transportation expenses, what software/systems the company uses, and the company's compensation and perquisite package. Time spent identifying and overcoming possible objections to your company's hiring parameters will save you time during your recruiting efforts. The two most common hiring parameters that affect recruiting efforts are location and compensation/perquisites. If you are a third-party recruiter, you have the additional challenge of identifying hiring parameters for every client you represent.

Location

If you are recruiting for position in which the employee needs to have an on-site presence every day, the company's location can either help or hurt your recruiting efforts. If your company is in a remote location, offers no public transportation, or requires a long commute, you will need to get creative and find new ways to recruit talent. One approach might be to research the profiles of current top employees and look to the talent of local adjacent industries in order to find talent. Once you establish a pipeline of local talent, you want to remain in regular contact with them so when they're ready to make a career move, they think of your company first.

Another way to attract top talent despite a limiting office location is to create a consistent and effective web and social media presence that highlights the best aspects of working at the company. Provide videos of employees talking about how great it is to work at your company. Turn your recruiting obstacle into an opportunity to attract top talent.

There are also employee transportation benefits that can be offered when your location is remote and there is limited transportation. Companies can offer a qualified transportation fringe benefit program to either set aside a pre-tax amount to cover vanpool costs or provide company funds to help cover the cost of commuting and deduct the costs as an employee benefit. Your company can also support ridesharing programs or partner with transportation providers to educate employees about alternative transportation options they could use to commute to work. In the case of high-level executive positions, your company could consider providing housing from

Monday to Friday with the employee commuting home on weekends. For low-level positions, you may consider utilizing a temporary staffing firm who often provide transportation for their employees if the volume is high enough to offset the costs of transportation.

Another option is to propose relocation. Often you can attract candidates from cities with a very high cost of living to a remote location by stressing the lower cost of living, better schools, housing, and other amenities. It's wise to partner with the local chamber of commerce, school district, and real estate professionals to explain the benefits of relocating to your location. It's also important to note that 84 percent of Millennials are willing to relocate for a job, and most are apartment dwellers, which simplifies the relocation process. In fact, 82 percent of Millennials believe they will be required to relocate if they want to advance their careers.

Lastly, suggest an annual evaluation of every position to determine if the job continues to require that candidates must work on-site. With so many advances in technology, many functions of jobs can be accomplished from home. If you can offer a combination of on-site and remote working hours, you will attract more top talent.

Compensation and perquisites

There are numerous factors to be considered when estimating the value of your company's entire compensation package. For example, if you are competing for scarce talent and your competitor offers a greater salary, you may still be able to attract candidates for whom other nonsalary benefits are more important. For example, benefits such as health insurance and/or family coverage, a cafeteria or other meal plan, contributions to retirement accounts, and cost coverage of any internal or external training can all be factored into a total compensation package.

Similarly, perks don't have to be big-ticket items. One of the most desirable perks in today's job market is a better work-life balance. Being able to work virtually and having flexible working hours are two of the top benefits valued by job seekers.[6] The good news is that employers benefit from flexible work arrangements as well. Many employers are realizing that flexible hours provide them with more coverage. They have employees who work 10:00 a.m. to 7:00 p.m. and others who work the traditional 8:00 a.m. to 5:00 p.m.

Company culture, while not considered compensation or a benefit, can play a major role in a candidate's decision when considering competing job offers. When I opened an office in Dallas, I was surprised by how many qualified candidates chose to work at Southwest Airlines, despite the fact that they were not the highest-paying employer in Dallas. These candidates chose Southwest for the company culture. Culture is so central to Southwest's operations that they even have a Culture Services Department that is charged with ensuring that every employee knows they matter. As Southwest Airlines explains, "Our Culture is woven into all aspects of our business and our Employees' lives, from the way Employees treat each other to the way that our Company puts our Employees first."[7] Southwest is even an active participant in the community, sponsoring locally hosted celebrations and recognition for life events and milestones.

Overcoming obstacles to your company's hiring parameters requires getting to know what your candidate values and communicating your company's value in a way that meets their needs. While we all need to money to pay the bills, there are benefits are that are more valuable to the right candidate than high compensation. Using a high-touch approach in recruiting can help you align both the needs of your company and the right candidate.

Performance objectives

Performance objectives outline the expected behaviors and metrics that define success in a specific role. Having clear performance objectives prevents recruiters from wasting their time by establishing the exact results that candidates need to achieve in order to be successful in that role. It also establishes clear performance expectations for potential candidates so they can quickly determine if they are interested and able to excel in the role.

Over ten years ago, when I began to obtain performance objectives, I realized there was a tremendous disconnect between the traditional job requisition I had obtained from my client and the skills needed to achieve the performance objectives. It's no different than an employer complaining their employees are not meeting their expectations, but they haven't shared exactly what they expect. I realized this could be one of the causes of disengagement and turnover. In order to obtain this additional information, I showed my hiring authorities how understanding performance objectives up front would improve the quality of candidate I could provide, and it will provide those same results for you.

Performance objectives will vary greatly depending on the level of position but should always clearly specify what a person must do to be successful. Table 1.3 contains eight guidelines to help you create performance objectives.

The best performance objectives are SMART—specific, measurable, achievable, relevant, and time-bound. They specify the problem

Table 1.3 Eight steps to writing performance objectives

Step 1	Identify six to eight major objectives.	Specify precisely what needs to be achieved to guarantee success.
Step 2	Confirm what is needed to achieve the major objectives.	Break down major objectives into two or three smaller goals.
Step 3	Identify what problems will be resolved.	Know what and how to resolve problems.
Step 4	Identify action items for each objective.	Create specific timeline.
Step 5	Describe team dynamics.	Outline and understand team dynamics that can help or hinder the attainment of performance objectives.
Step 6	Determine priorities and time frame.	Review action items and determine priorities and deadlines.
Step 7	Define short-term goals.	Consider long-term goals while determining short-term goals that must be achieved.
Step 8	Define long-term goals.	Set time frame to achieve long-term goals which involve strategic thinking and implementation.

that is being addressed, how to address the problem, establish a timeline for deliverable(s), and outline how success will be measured. Using the job description in Table 1.2, consider how you might strengthen the performance objectives for the Talent Partner position at Gradient Ventures. See Table 1.4 for a suggested revision.

Providing a high level of specificity and detail in writing performance objectives saves time in the overall hiring process and helps eliminate any and all confusion as to what it means to be successful. It helps the recruiter limit their search to only those with the right credentials and track record that proves they could achieve the objectives. It helps the candidate understand exactly what they need to do

Table 1.4 Suggested revision to performance objectives for talent partner at Gradient Ventures[8]

V1. Performance Objectives	V2. SMART Performance Objectives
1. Assess Talent Needs	
Across Gradient's portfolio companies, understand the specific nuances and culture of each organization and, in collaboration with the entrepreneurs, drive outcomes that change the trajectory of a company.	Meet with entrepreneur to identify nuances and culture of each organization. Conduct a GAP analysis to determine current reality versus key hiring objectives. Prioritize outcomes that will change the trajectory of each company. Understand strategies to implement in order to accomplish their objectives that most affect company goals. Obtain specific target dates to hire.
2. Create and Lead a Talent Program	
Focus on identifying and forming a strong perspective on the next-generation set of AI entrepreneurs, companies, and executive talent for the Gradient portfolio.	

(continued)

Table 1.4 (Continued)

3. Set an Executive Talent Strategy	
Leverage your knowledge of HR/Talent, operations and venture capital and/or private equity space to set and execute talent strategy and influence founders and senior leadership.	Conduct research to identify and form a strong perspective on the next-gen. Identify AI entrepreneurs and companies. Also identify executive talent for the Gradient portfolio. Submit results monthly including proposed follow-up action items.
4. Gradient's Operational Strategy	
Help develop and execute Gradient's operational strategy	Share your knowledge of HR, talent, operations, and the venture capital and/or private equity space with founders and senior leadership. Utilize data to be included in the company's executive talent strategy to influence decisions reached by senior leadership. Present recommendations on a monthly basis and track results of talent strategies implemented.
5. Lead Community Engagement	
Lead community engagement initiatives and expansion of Gradient's core team and portfolio companies.	Help develop Gradient's operational strategy that describes how we will employ resources to support our corporate strategy. Once developed, create timelines for completion of the strategies outlined.

to be considered a high performer so they can quickly decide whether they are interested or not. And, down the road, it gives the hiring manager a means to assess new employee performance.

Interview process

The interview process is one of the most important aspects of the hiring process as it allows the company to connect and better evaluate job candidates and, in turn, allows candidates to see if the company is a good match for their skills and interests. While the interview process needs to be comprehensive in order to be effective, in a competitive job market it is imperative that candidates can move through the process quickly and efficiently. Technology has played a key role in helping speed up the interviewing process; helping companies save time and money by conducting early interviews via videoconference, Skype, or phone; and then storing feedback and scheduling details in either your applicant tracking systems (ATS) or client relationship management system (CRM).

One of the biggest questions that hiring authorities struggle with is determining the length of the interview process. I've had clients extend a job offer after one interview, and I've had other clients conduct eight interviews. Then I heard about the "Rule of Four" that originated at Google. Google is a company consistently ranked as one of the top companies desired by candidates, receiving over three million applications per year with only 0.2 percent of candidates getting hired. Google established the Rule of Four as a best practice after analyzing a subset of interview data collected for over five years to determine the value of a single interviewer's feedback. The research showed that "four interviews were enough to predict whether someone should be hired."[9] Reducing interviews to four rounds has reduced their average time to hire by almost two weeks, saving employees "hundreds of hours in interviewing time," according to Sharon Shaper, Google's Hiring Innovation Manager.[10]

To keep your candidate engaged and interested, it's important to suggest limiting your interviewing process to four rounds. You may not personally be able to facilitate this change, but you can initiate conversations that prove to your hiring managers that they are losing talent and money when an interview process is too long. The four rounds of interviews generally include a phone interview, a panel interview with a hiring manager and peers, an in-person "day at the job," and the final interview with the hiring manager.

When a four-round interviewing process is embraced, make sure that everyone involved—including the candidate—understands the objective of each round of interviews. For example, during the initial phone interview, the recruiter's objective is to determine if a candidate is qualified and should be recommended for a second interview. They are providing a high-level overview of the role and the company while also evaluating the candidate's communication skills, competency, and interest level. At this stage, the recruiter wants to discover any red flags—either in the candidate's history or in any of the hiring parameters or performance objectives that may cause the candidate to be screened out. By making it clear to the candidate what the objective is at the beginning of the phone interview, the recruiter can keep the interview focused and decide whether that candidate can move to the next round.

The second interview is the panel interview. In the panel interview, the candidate is interviewed by a maximum of four people who will directly or indirectly interact with the candidate should they be hired. They all share a vested interest in hiring the best person for the job. The purpose of the panel interview is to allow multiple people to provide input and feedback on the candidate.

If the candidate is screened in, the third interview which is a job audition, is scheduled. The purpose of the job audition is to help candidates visualize themselves in the role by seeing it done firsthand. In my own company, I have found the job audition to be critical in hiring the best talent. After hiring salespeople for years, I realized that hearing about a job was very different than seeing a job performed. When interviewing new recruiters, we asked them to watch our current recruiting team make presentations to prospective candidates. It's amazing how many prospective hires are surprised by the level of rejection, obstacles, and objections our recruiters experience. Many candidates also find themselves learning that there are candidates who would rather speak to a recruiter by phone instead of being sent an email or a text. The job audition is a critical step in my hiring process that has helped me to eliminate bad hires.

The final interview is conducted by the prospective hire's manager. The purpose of this interview is for the manager to determine if this person aligns with the company culture, core values, department, and current team members. At the same time, it allows the candidate to clarify any areas of concerns so they can ensure the position, company, culture, etc., are a good fit for them.

Candidate appraisal

I recommend creating a candidate assessment process in order to quantify answers and remove emotion and bias from the decision-making process. If done properly the candidate appraisal process will not only help you find the right candidate but will also provide the candidate's future supervisor with great insight into the candidate after they are hired.

I suggest using an interview scorecard for each position (see Figure 1.1) that outlines the performance objectives, technical skills,

Figure 1.1 Interview scorecard

INTERVIEW SCORECARD

Candidate name: _____ Date: _____
Position interviewed for: _____
Name of interviewer: _____

Rank the candidate using a scale of 1 to 5 (5 being highest)

Criteria	Interview rating (1–5)	After-hire performance (1–5)	Gap	Action items
Performance objective #1				
Performance objective #2				
Performance objective #3				
Performance objective #4				
Performance objective #5				
Performance objective #6				
Technical ability				
Soft skill examples:				
• Communication				
• Interpersonal/team				
• Organizational				
• Problem solving				

TOTAL:
AVERAGE RATING:

Figure 1.1 (Continued)

Rating definitions:

5 – Candidate is well versed in this area and will need little or no training
4 – Candidate has done similar work, but minimal experience in this area
3 – Candidate can do the work, but will need training
2 – Candidate lacks this experience or skill
1 – Unqualified

Candidates who average a 3 or less should be eliminated from consideration

Additional interview notes:

Concerns:

and soft skills required for a job. The information on the scorecard will differ based on the performance objectives and characteristics needed for each position. I use a 1 to 5 ratings scale to simplify scoring and define what each number rating means so that everyone involved in the interviewing process is using the same rating system. (I've found that using a common language and appraisal system helps fine-tune your teams' ability to interview and assess talent.) Your scorecard should also include a section for notes where interviewers can indicate a strength, skill, or talent the candidate possessed that is not addressed by the scorecard but that could be useful in this position. You should also have a section for concerns where interviewers can mention any unusual body language or evasive answers.

Once performance objectives, technical, and soft skills have been identified, they are listed on the left column of the scorecard. Everyone involved in the interviewing process rates each candidate in all categories. Scores are added up and divided by the number of items listed in the criteria column to calculate an average score for each candidate.

During the debrief session after the panel interview, members of the panel can revise their scores based on input from other panel members. Revisions can only be made before the scorecard is submitted and scores are entered into the applicant tracking system.

The scorecard accomplishes two things pre-hire. It rates the candidate during interviews and helps you hire talent that has the best chance of success. The scorecard also accomplishes three things post-hire. It helps rate performance after the hire, identifies gaps in the interviewing or hiring process, and helps identify additional actions or training that is needed.

Summary

You now understand how the hiring process can either enhance or hinder your recruiting efforts. You are under pressure to fill open requisitions but now realize how important it is to initiate actions needed to update hiring processes. Take time to review the five aspects that waste the most time, energy, and money in the hiring process and share this information with your hiring managers including: job requisitions, hiring parameters, performance objectives, interview process, and candidate appraisal. Show your hiring managers that their current hiring process could be costing them money or causing them to lose the top talent they prefer to hire.

If you can only facilitate one change, I would suggest you include performance standards on every requisition. Knowing how your candidates will be evaluated and deemed successful in their role will guide your recruiting efforts. This will also improve the engagement and retention of the candidates you represent, which benefits your hiring managers, candidates, and you.

Your interview process should be limited to no more than four interviews, if you want to attract top talent. The next most important change to consider is combining multiple interviews into a panel interview, where you obtain a group consensus on candidates which also alleviates bias.

Key takeaways

- The job requisition should be updated and identify what an organization requires but should also provide a sense of the company culture and opportunities for professional growth.

- Before you begin to create or revise a job requisition, ask the hiring manager one very important question: "How will this person be evaluated at the end of six months or at the end of a year?" Keep this information in the forefront when writing your job requisition.

- Writing job requisitions that lead to recruiting engaged employees is not only critical for you as a recruiter, but critical to the long-term success of the hiring authority. The costs of employee turnover are enormous. Each departure costs approximately one-third of that worker's annual earnings.

- Two hiring parameters that most affect your recruiting efforts are location and compensation/perquisites. Learning how to overcome possible objections to your company's hiring parameters will save you time during your recruiting efforts.

- Company culture, while not considered compensation or a benefit, can play a major role in a candidate's decision when considering competing job offers.

- Save time by obtaining performance objectives which establish the exact criteria the candidates you place need to have to become successful.

- The interview process is one of the most important aspects of the hiring process as it allows the organization to connect and better evaluate job candidates and, in turn, allows candidates to see if the organization is a good match for their skills and interests.

- The interview process should be comprehensive to identify the best talent but must also be efficient with no more than four rounds of interviews. Everyone involved in the interview process should understand the objective of each round of interviews, including the candidate.

- Creating and utilizing a scorecard can help appraise candidates while also eliminating bias and emotion from hiring decisions. Once candidates are hired, the interview scorecard can help rate employee performance, identify gaps in the interviewing or hiring process, and help identify additional actions or training that is needed.

- Review the five aspects of the hiring process and select the one that will have the greatest impact on your recruiting efforts. Present your recommendations, stressing how a high-tech high-touch approach to your hiring process will attract the best talent, reduce your time to hire, and result in more offers that are accepted.

- After changes have been made to the hiring process, review the results at least annually.

- Make additional changes to consistently improve.

Endnotes

1 Josh Bersin, "Google for Jobs: Potential to Disrupt the $200 Billion Recruiting Industry," *Forbes*, May 25, 2017, https://joshbersin.com/2017/05/google-for-jobs-disrupting-the-recruiting-market/ (archived at https://perma.cc/5GM4-XNP7)

2 Tom Popomaronis, "Here's How Many Google Interviews It Takes to Hire a Googler," CNBC Make It, April 17, 2019, https://www.cnbc.com/2019/04/17/heres-how-many-google-job-interviews-it-takes-to-hire-a-googler.html (archived at https://perma.cc/2HN3-FRZY)

3 Theresa Agovino, "To Have and to Hold," SHRM, February 23, 2019, https://www.shrm.org/hr-today/news/all-things-work/pages/to-have-and-to-hold.aspx (archived at https://perma.cc/3597-RZB7)

4 Josh Linkner, "The 21 Most Creative Titles," *Forbes*, December 4, 2014, https://www.forbes.com/sites/joshlilnkner/2014/12/04/the-21-most-creative-job-titles/#448c0a322933 (archived at https://perma.cc/U7TV-NB4M)

5 Linkner, "The 21 Most Creative Job Titles."

6 "Employee Benefits Study: The Cost and Value of Employee Perks," Fractl, April 16, 2020, http://www.frac.tl/employee-benefits-study/ (archived at https://perma.cc/T22G-LZHB)

7 Southwest Careers, "Culture," 2020, https://careers.southwestair.com/culture (archived at https://perma.cc/42ZG-UTMW)

8 Job Description—Talent Partner—Gradient Ventures.

9 Popomaronis, "Here's How Many Google Interviews It Takes to Hire a Googler."

10 Popomaronis, "Here's How Many Google Interviews It Takes to Hire a Googler."

Identify the best talent and communicate effectively

2

Successful recruiters know how to recognize high performers, where to find them, and how to determine if their interests align with available job requisitions. Finding high-potential employees requires more than using a search algorithm and a keyword search for "high performer." They know how to successfully balance the use of sophisticated search engines combined with their own high-touch recruiting skills in order to unearth those candidates who are the right fit for the role and company. They initially suggest a conversation to discuss what the candidate feels is their next career move before presenting a specific job. This also eliminates questions that may be slanted toward the specifications of an open requisition. During this conversation, recruiters need to know what differentiates the best talent from simply average candidates. As with all other aspects of recruiting, identifying the best talent and communicating with them effectively requires a high-tech, high-touch approach.

How to recognize top talent

Technology has made it quicker and easier to find candidates who match specific criteria and job requirements. LinkedIn Recruiter allows you to search the entire database of LinkedIn members (over

500 million at present) and use set filters to select those candidates who are the best match.[1] Once you've collected this pool of candidates, you can then review individual profiles to find those candidates whose profiles seem the most promising.

You can also identify potential candidates using both Twitter and Facebook. If you follow the right industries, people, and hashtags, Twitter can be an excellent way to find and recruit top talent. A staggering 61 percent of job seekers use Twitter as part of their job search.[2] To get the best result use the advanced search interface to help with your recruiting efforts. This will allow you to leverage hashtags, geocoding, and RSS feeds on Twitter so you can narrow down the field and locate the best candidates, even for hard-to-fill positions like software engineers or .net developers. This allows you to filter out candidates by location and specific skill sets far more easily than searching hashtags alone. To use the advanced search, there are four steps. First, enter your search into the search bar on Twitter.com. Second, click advanced search, located below search filters on the upper right of your results page, or click More Options and then click on advanced search. Third, fill in the appropriate fields to refine your search results, and fourth, click Search to view your results.

Following candidates is a great way to see if candidates will fit into your company culture and to learn more about them before your first contact. Once you've identified a potential candidate on Twitter, utilize what you've learned about them by looking at their Twitter profile and their tweets. It is to your advantage to then reach out to them with a personalized tweet. Rather than pitching a job, suggest an offline discussion about what they envision as their next career move.

The best way to recruit talent utilizing Twitter is to build a strong presence. Tweet often, tweet about subjects that represent the professions you're recruiting for, and interact daily with people in those professions. Set up a separate account just for recruiting so you can easily stream out prospective candidates from general followers.

Most people are on Facebook to stay in touch with family and friends. Facebook also makes it simple to connect in groups with people who have common interests. When someone is conducting a job search, they are likely to join job search groups in their location or area of expertise. Facebook is a great platform to engage in conversations with these passive candidates about similar interests. Facebook also makes it relatively simple to search through industry-specific groups for qualified talent. Individuals who use Facebook will not hesitate to tag their friends when they see a new job opportunity.

If you want to invest some of your recruiting budget in advertising, you can also run ads on Facebook which can target specific job titles, experience, education, interests, and location. If you decide to invest in paid advertising, it's wise to track the return on this investment.

Once you have your pool of potential candidates, you need to separate the best talent from the simply average candidates (see Table 2.1). This process involves reviewing their entire profile, not just their past work experience. Peak performers are more likely to participate in specific interest groups, post articles or blogs that reflect their expertise, and comment on other posts. They will have received recognition or awards throughout their life and have recommendations from peers or former managers. In reviewing recommendations or skills, look for keywords such as "critical thinker," "competitive," "conscientious," and "creative problem solver."

You'll want to see if they are members of professional associations and, if so, whether they are in a leadership role. Most associations post their membership lists, board of directors, and committee heads online, so you can easily identify and reach out to these high achievers. You may even consider attending an association meeting (if it's convenient) to meet them in person, which also provides an opportunity to meet additional high achievers.

Where to find top talent

Many companies begin their recruiting process by posting open positions on job boards hosted by data aggregators like Monster and Indeed. They may also post their opportunities on websites like LinkedIn. While posting on job boards and websites assures you that a large number of people will view your position, it is also expensive

Table 2.1 Characteristics of best hires

Adaptable	Adapts to change and unexpected challenges
Communicator	Uses written and verbal skills to help team accomplish goals without offending others
Value-aligned	Creates, supports, and works toward goals that align with company core values
Achievement-oriented	Completes key tasks on time, accurately, and under budget. Has track record of consistently going above and beyond what is expected
Dependable	Willing to do what it takes to get job done, often the "go to" person in times of difficulty or in high-pressure situations
Detail-oriented	Notices important details without getting bogged down by little things, prevents problems from surfacing later that could sabotage projects
Disciplined	Has determination, focus, and initiative to drive projects and complete tasks by deadlines
Driven	Always motivated to do their best
High energy	Enthusiastic, dynamic, and positive; inspires and motivates team members
Honest	Speaks the truth with compassion
Resilient	Works well under pressure and learns from failures
Curious	Asks questions and looks for new opportunities and possibilities in existing systems/products
Entrepreneurial	Takes initiative, anticipates trends, and willingly assumes leadership of new initiatives. Has a track record of completing projects successfully
Motivates and inspires others	Brings out the best in those around them, inspires others to follow their lead
Learning mindset	Embraces failures as opportunity to learn and grow, seeks out career development and training opportunities
Positive	Optimistic and able to envision the end game regardless of challenges and obstacles

(continued)

Table 2.1 (Continued)

Professional	Conducts themselves appropriately, quick to comprehend office culture and customs
Respectful	Treats others the way they want to be treated
Team-oriented	Collaborates and respects talents and skills of team members
Tech-savvy	Embraces new technologies

and generally doesn't result in attracting the best candidates. Companies spend almost $2.5 billion a year on these kinds of ads and only reach 15 percent of the available talent.

You have the unique opportunity to bring added high-touch value to the hiring authority by identifying passive candidates. These are top performers who are currently working and successful but also might consider a new opportunity if it represented a good career move. Passive candidates represent a far greater percentage—namely 85 percent—of the available talent for your position, and they are not looking at job boards or website postings. However, most of them do not intend to retire from their current place of employment.

Hiring authorities are also a great resource for identifying high-potential, passive candidates. Hiring authorities are well networked and are often aware of outstanding individuals in their field whom they would hire without hesitation. They can easily identify candidates who have a reputation of peak performance. Even if they do not have specific individuals to recommend, hiring authorities can usually suggest companies for you to target. Again, because they are a part of the industry, they know which companies (besides their own) hire the best people. Just as important, ask your hiring authority for the names of individuals or companies *not* to target. After all, you don't want to spend time targeting and interviewing individuals that your hiring authorities will screen out.

Another way to identify passive talent is by reaching out to your candidate network and ask for referrals. If you helped place a candidate in a new role and company that represented career advancement and they are thriving, they are more apt to be willing to provide you with referrals. Ask if they could share the names of any peak performers from their last company who are successfully working in a job that is similar to the job you are attempting to fill. Be careful about how you ask, though. If you ask someone who is working "who they know" or if they can "provide you with referrals of top talent," you will almost always hear, "I don't know anyone!" Instead, you should ask, "Who is the best (job title) from your last place of employment?" This prevents the response "I don't know anyone," because they most certainly remember the best people from their last place of employment.

The reason most people respond with "I don't know anyone" is they assume you are asking for names of their current coworkers and that makes them uncomfortable, because they are loyal to their current employer. However, most people feel comfortable providing you with names of coworkers from their past employer because they don't have the same level of loyalty. If your conversation is moving along smoothly, continue to ask them for the names of high performers from all their past employers. In the future if you hear the response "I don't know anyone," you now realize you asked them the wrong question.

As a general practice, it is wise to keep your network informed about new opportunities so they can easily refer qualified candidates to you. Send bimonthly emails which include a relevant article, a compelling subject line, and a list of current jobs you are trying to fill. Most emails are not opened, so pay special attention when writing your subject line. It must be a topic that is relevant. When candidates receive information from you including a sample list of your current job opportunities, they will be more likely to forward your email to their address book, which results in additional talent reaching out to you.

To obtain referrals, you are competing with internal referral programs and other bonuses. For this reason, it's imperative that you set up a referral program so that candidates benefit by referring top talent to you versus someone else. People do things for their own reasons, and if they personally benefit by sending you referrals, they are more likely to participate in your referral program.

Communicate effectively to engage top talent

Recruiters face an uphill battle in getting the attention of candidates and hiring authorities. In order to stand out, always work on improving your communication skills. How you communicate is as important as what you are saying. While most recruiters feel they communicate clearly, many realize after conflicts or frustrating events that the person they were speaking with heard something totally different from what they said. The recruiter's message was lost because they didn't communicate effectively.

Recruiting is about building relationships with hiring authorities and candidates. As the conduit between the candidate and the hiring manager, you need to be clear in both your verbal and nonverbal communication as well as a keen listener to the needs of both parties. Effective communication is so much more than simply exchanging information. It's being able to understand the relevance, emotion, and intention behind the information being shared. It's also the ability to make the other person feel heard and understood.

The most successful recruiters have mastered the skills that allow them to effectively communicate. The following are some best practices that I've found to be invaluable in my career.

Focus and be present

An important part of communicating respectfully is eliminating all distractions. People can tell when you're not fully attentive. When you're on the phone or in a meeting with your candidate or client, allow yourself to be focused solely on the conversation.

If you are meeting someone in person, turn off your phone and make sure everyone in your office is aware you're in a meeting and not to be disturbed. If you allow yourself to be interrupted, the person in your office does not feel like a priority, which will eliminate your ability to develop rapport and trust. Take notes so you can refer to them during future conversations with your candidate and client.

If the meeting is taking place in someone else's office, you can learn a tremendous amount of information about this person by looking around. Notice diplomas or certifications, personal pictures, sports memorabilia, or anything else that provides you with personal insight. When you can get another person to talk about something that they enjoy first, they will like you more without realizing why. Most people would rather talk about the weather, sports, or just about anything else rather than listen to your pitch. This is the reason it's important not to sell before you know what's most important to each person.

People like to buy, but they don't like to be sold. If you are talking to a candidate, you can't discuss a potential job opportunity until you understand what they see as their next career move. If you're in the office of a hiring manager or prospective client (if you're a third-party recruiter), you need to understand their challenges before you can position yourself as a solution. To accomplish this, the conversation needs to have your undivided attention, which helps you to establish rapport and trust.

Listen

When you are present and focused, you are better able to listen and to ensure your own understanding of what is being said. Rather than interrupting in an effort to be heard, focus on trying to understand and appreciate what your client or candidate is trying to say. Listen to understand where they are coming from instead of listening to solve their problem.

Some people do not have anyone in their life who listens to understand rather than judge them or provide solutions. Share with your candidates and hiring managers that your goal is to become the best listener in their life. When I ask clients, candidates, or recruiters to name the best listener in their life, the most common answers are "my mother," "my best friend" (if they don't have a bigger agenda), "my spouse," and "my dog." When you clarify your understanding of words used, repeat what a client or candidate has shared with you, and focus on what is most important to them, you are demonstrating your ability to listen.

When you understand their perspective and what they want and need, you will make better matches resulting in employee engagement and retention. This will establish long-term working relationships with both your hiring managers and candidates based on trust and, as a result, will fill more requisitions.

Look for nonverbal cues

Being a good listener forces you to pay attention to little but important things, like voice inflection or, when you're speaking face-to-face, nonverbal cues. When utilizing tools like Skype or a webcam to interview, try to observe facial expressions, eye contact, and posture. While body language often serves to reinforce the words being spoken, it can also signal whether something is wrong or if the person is not being truthful. While speaking with hiring authorities and candidates, make sure your body language and posture convey your interest and appreciation for what is being said. You also need to listen and pay attention to what candidates and hiring authorities are verbally and nonverbally communicating so you can fully understand the relevance, emotion, and intentions behind information being shared. As a recruiter, your reputation is dependent on finding the best matches, so if someone's body language isn't matching what they are saying, it's critical to ask questions again in a future follow-up contact to clarify their answers.

Let's review body language that will help you observe both positive and negative nonverbal cues. A candidate's nonverbal cues begin with their handshake, which should be firm but not crushing. The "wet fish" handshake does not project a good first impression. Next, it's important for a candidate to make eye contact during your interview, but not constant eye contact, which can project aggression. However, a lack of eye contact can project dishonesty.

Next let's address posture and sitting style. A candidate should sit up straight and avoid slumping in a chair. If you notice that they lean forward slightly, that is an indicator of interest. If they recline back into the chair fully, this can give an impression of boredom or disengagement in the interview. If a candidate crosses their arms, this can indicate defensiveness, nerves, and a need for self-protection. You ideally want them to convey confidence during an interview. If candidates fidget, bite their nails, twirl their hair, or tap their foot, these gestures are generally considered impolite, appear unprofessional, and convey a high level of nerves.

If your candidate naturally talks with their hands you don't want them to stop, because this could lead to them appearing awkward during their interview. However, their hand motions should not distract from what they are saying. Paying close attention to body language could possibly surface additional red flags that you will want to address when you are checking references with past supervisors.

Prioritize your candidate's needs

Early in your recruiting process, you have an opportunity to determine the needs of your prospective candidates. Determine if this person can talk openly to you during business hours or if this person needs to talk when they are at home during evening or weekend hours. Most candidates do *not* have a private office and are unable to talk openly at work. However, they may be willing to talk with you when they get home from work. In this instance, ask for their cell phone number and hang up. This shows candidates that you are willing to work around their schedule, and it helps you achieve a great first impression. Interviewing after hours will differentiate you from recruiters who are not willing to make calls after regular working hours.

The interviewing process is about self-reflection, and all candidates have preferences that align with their needs and wants. Most candidates prefer a certain type of career in a specific location within the salary range they desire. Some candidates will not consider relocation because they want to be near their family, while others want to experience a new part of the country or world. Overall, most candidates want to accept a new opportunity with a company that allows them to be themselves.

List the factors that are most important to each candidate and determine if each represents a must-have (needs), a could-live-with or -without (wants), or a deal-breaker (absolute no). Then ask your candidate to help you list the factors in order of their priority. For example, you might have a candidate who prefers to work in Florida, but you find out they had turned down three previous offers in Florida because of money. In this example, the *need* of earning more money outweighed the *want* to move to Florida. Moving to Florida is still a factor but would be listed lower on the list of priorities. When you walk your candidate through this process, it helps them determine what they need and what they want. They appreciate the fact that you're helping them understand what is most important to them. This process will also help you make better matches for them that result in offers they will accept.

Ask questions

The best recruiters in our profession have mastered the ability to ask the best questions and clarify the responses. Here's an example where curiosity can be beneficial. You ask a candidate, "What is most important for you to consider a career change?" and your candidate simply answers, "Advancement." As an experienced recruiter, you know that advancement can mean many different things. It could mean more money, a higher-level position, an expansion of their current job scope, or even simply the opportunity to advance faster at their current company. The only way you can find out what your candidate means by advancement is to ask them the following question: "What is your definition of advancement?"

Before you can help your candidate find a job that meets their needs, you must make sure that you ask the questions that help clarify their needs. Make sure you ask your candidate (and hiring authority) for clarification when they use words that are subject to interpretation based on the person who is speaking. Words or phrases such as "advancement," "benefits," or "good opportunity" can mean different things based on who is speaking. Ask questions to make sure you understand exactly what is being communicated.

My office was in downtown Chicago, and often candidates would specify the number of blocks they were willing to walk from their bus or train to their job. Winter in Chicago can be brutal between the snow and winds. During an interview, I asked my candidate how far she was willing to walk to her job, and she said five blocks from the South Shore Train Station. I asked the question, listened to her answer, but still proceeded to send her on a job interview six blocks from her train station. The hiring manager felt she was the perfect fit for their company and the job, she expressed a high level of interest in the job, and the compensation package was much higher than anticipated. She initially accepted the job offer and then two days later declined the offer because it was further than she wanted to walk. I asked her the question, but then I ignored her answer. This wasted her time, my client's time, and my time as well.

Relate to others

In the recruiting profession you will interact with new people every day, which is why it's important to effectively relate to others. You may be totally different than the candidates you represent, but that's not important. What is important is that you put yourself in their shoes and see the world through their eyes. Make them feel relevant and explain that you want to become the best listener in their lives. Never forget, every person you approach wants to know one thing, "WIIFM": What's in it for me if we continue this discussion?

Very early in your conversation, ask questions that allow the other person to talk about themselves. When you let someone talk about themselves, they tend to like you more without realizing why. Show a true interest in what they are saying, and ask questions to allow them to delve even deeper into topics most important to them. This proves you really want to clarify and understand what they are sharing. If you have any common interests like sports, schools attended, community involvement, or hobbies, share them with your candidate to become even more relatable.

The ability to relate is crucial when you are working with hiring authorities or candidates in areas where you have little or no expertise. For example, while you may not have the skills to be a software engineer, you need to be able to relate to candidates who are software engineers. You need to figure out what they want and whether their needs match the requirements for the requisitions you are attempting to fill.

Relating to others is about finding common ground, realizing and accepting what you don't know, and most importantly, being open to new information. Show genuine interest in learning more about the other person, and accept that you don't have to like or agree with everyone; you just have to relate to them, so you can establish rapport that will eventually lead to trust.

Relating across multiple generations

In any given day, the candidates you're recruiting and the hiring authorities you're working with could span all generations, from Baby Boomers through Generation Z. Knowing something about their communication style will help you relate to them more effectively. For example, Baby Boomers are those individuals born between 1946 and 1964 and grew up in a very different workplace, so their communication preferences might be different than yours. In my experience, I find that Baby Boomers prefer a mix of communication by email, voicemail, face-to-face conversations, and meetings. Generation X, born between 1965 and 1980, strive for a better work-life balance than Baby Boomers, and in my experience prefer to be contacted about work issues during work hours. Email is the form of communication they prefer, and they want face-to-face meetings kept to a minimum. Millennials, born between 1981 and 1996, are the driving force behind many changes in current communication styles. They grew up on the internet, are almost always connected, and are extremely tech-savvy. Millennials have a heavy reliance on electronic means of communicating, and require prompt feedback and meaningful interaction. Generation Z, born between 1995 and 2012, expect information to be instantly available. They can take in information instantaneously but can lose interest just as fast. Communication with these individuals needs to be concise and visual. Generation Z communicates with images, and they multitask across multiple screens. They also prefer video and images to text. However, personalization is the key to grabbing the attention of Generation Z. When you're communicating with a prospective recruit, don't underestimate the value of a face-to-face meeting.

If you want to represent the best talent from every generation, communicate in the way that is preferred and most effective. On the other side of the recruiting process, you must also determine the most effective and preferred way to communicate with your hiring authorities.

Speak authoritatively

The way you speak matters, and in the recruiting profession it's important to speak with confidence and authority, which will inspire respect from both your hiring authorities and candidates. Hiring authorities depend on you to help them and their company achieve goals and objectives. Candidates trust you to help them advance their career, which is a tremendous responsibility. Both your hiring authorities and candidates want to be represented by an authority whom they can trust.

Being prepared and knowing what you are talking about is necessary, but sometimes you don't have the opportunity to prepare a response in advance. For example, if someone is complaining about a bad experience they had with another recruiter, you should respond with empathy by listening to them and hearing them voice their concerns. Speak slowly and clearly after listening, and ask open-ended questions to allow the upset party to be heard. When you respond, the person must feel that you have their best interests at heart and will do whatever you can to solve the issue.

If a candidate or client asks you for your opinion or advice, always base your response on facts and not emotion. In most instances neither of them actually want your opinion; they are using you as their sounding board because they trust you as a workforce/workplace expert. When you respond, focus on how they will benefit from your advice and try to provide more than one option, always asking them for input on what they feel is best.

Use the right communication tool for the situation

Technology has changed the way recruiters communicate with both their candidates and clients. Texting is a great way to confirm interviews, but it's not the right tool to have a meaningful conversation about a candidate's career goals. While email may be a great way to introduce yourself and provide some detail on how you work with other hiring authorities, you don't want to base an entire recruiting relationship on email alone. The harsh reality is that most emails are never opened.

In order to choose the appropriate communication tool, be clear on what it is you are trying to accomplish. If you're looking to confirm an appointment or need just a quick yes or no answer, texting is fine. If you need to provide more detailed information that requires an explanation, an email can suffice. If it's a formal job offer, you should schedule a phone call, followed by a version in email format (for a quick response), and/or even a written letter sent by mail. If you need to discuss a personal matter that is highly sensitive, or if you want to gauge someone's interest in a position, you need a more personal form of communication. This should be a phone or video call, so that you can better read their body language and assess non-verbal cues.

Also keep in mind that the right communication tool may differ as you communicate with the different generations in the workplace.

Putting it all together: recruiting passive candidates

One of the most important decisions a person makes is a career move. The decision to change jobs or careers impacts the quality of a candidate's life, their earning and advancement potential, and their future marketability. As a recruiter, you need to be aware of the risk involved when asking someone to leave a role in which they are successful. If you recruit a passive candidate who is successful at their current job, you are asking them to trust you with their future. If you don't do your job properly, you may negatively impact their career and future marketability. You have a moral and ethical responsibility to do the best job you can for every candidate you recruit. If they accept a new opportunity, this decision not only affects them, it also affects their family and the other people in their lives. We spend most of our waking hours at work, which is why changing jobs has such a tremendous impact on the candidates you represent.

At the same time, I have found that most people don't intend to retire from their current job and are often open to hearing about new opportunities. However, before presenting a candidate with a new opportunity, make sure you do your homework. Review their LinkedIn profile and learn as much as you can about them before reaching out. Once you reach them by phone, refrain from selling or pitching a specific opportunity until you know what is most important to each prospective candidate. It's also important that you don't assume that what they're currently doing is what they want to do next, which is one of the biggest mistakes most recruiters make.

Reaching out to passive candidates

Like anything else in life, recruiting pitches get better with practice. I've been a recruiter for most of my career, and I still make recruiting presentations every day. Here are two general recruiting scripts to help you reach out to passive candidates.

General recruiting script 1

"Good morning/afternoon, _____. My name is _____, and I represent the best (IT/banking/financial services) employers in (geographic area.) In the past few months, we've placed several outstanding (insert job title) with similar experience to yours, and they're doing extremely well, which is why I'm reaching out to you.

"When would it be most convenient to discuss what's most important to you in your next career move?"

General recruiting script 2

"Good morning, _____. My name is _____.

"I was inspired to call you when I reviewed your résumé/LinkedIn. You have outstanding experience, and I've helped several candidates with similar experience advance their careers in great companies. I don't want to assume what you're doing is what you want to do next, so when would it be best for us to continue this discussion?"

If a candidate was referred to you, you will want to use the name of the person who referred them, as indicated in the Referred Candidate Script.

Referred candidate script

"Good morning/afternoon. My name is _____, and I was referred to you by _____. I work for the best (IT/banking/financial services firms), and we are always attempting to attract the best talent, which is why the people we place are retained. When I asked _____ for the name of the best (job title) at his/her last place of employment, you were the first person he mentioned. In fact, he shared that you (share info).

"I'd love to arrange a time when we can talk so I could understand what is most important to you in your next career move."

If the candidate expresses interest, set up a time in the evening to fully interview the candidate. Obtain detailed information and know the hot buttons of the candidate before presenting an opportunity. If you present the right type of opportunity, you will gain the trust and interest of this new candidate. If you have nothing that fits, tell them that you will contact them when the opportunity they describe crosses your desk. Assure them that you will not waste their time and that your process is confidential, so you will not jeopardize their current job. If you're a third-party recruiter, you could offer to market their skills to some of your best clients or to companies they most prefer.

If the candidate isn't interested in speaking further, tell them you would still like to get to know them for any future needs they may have. When a candidate says no to your recruiting efforts, they are really saying not yet. Even though they may not be interested now, they may be interested in another opportunity in the future. Add them to your candidate network and keep them informed of current opportunities.

Overcoming objections is a crucial part of a recruiter's job. How you handle objections is what separates the successful recruiter from the rest. Rather than viewing candidate objections as barriers to success, treat them as requests for more information. The only objection you can't overcome is silence. As long as your prospect is still talking to you, there is a good chance you can turn them into a recruited candidate.

It helps to realize there are only four categories of objections. When you can identify the type of objection you are receiving, it's much easier to effectively overcome it. The four categories of objections are price, personal, postponement, and service. A price objection is when the candidate is concerned you will not extend an adequate compensation package. A personal objection is when someone may have interacted with you in the past and had a negative experience. A postponement objection is any objection that delays your process. A service objection is when a candidate puts all recruiters in the same category and feels they don't need your services to find their next opportunity.

For any objection, you first want to confirm your understanding of their objection, and let the candidate know you heard them and understand why they might feel that way. Even though they may not be interested right now, you want to take this opportunity to let them know how you can help them when they are ready to make a career move.

Overcoming common objections

There are some common objections that can be overcome if you can keep the conversation going. Here are four common objections with some responses you can use to help improve your chances of representing these prospective candidates.

"I'm not looking for another job."

Try responding with "That's not a problem, the last five people with your background who I helped advance their career were also working and not looking for another job." Or you can say "My client is looking to hire individuals who have a great track record but might be open to a new job that represents their next career move. What do you see as your next career move?"

"You're the third recruiter who has called me today."

An effective response could be "That is such a compliment to you. We all want to represent the best talent in the market, and that's why you're receiving these calls. I've helped 10 individuals with your experience advance their careers in the last 90 days. What do you see as your next career move?"

"I don't have time to talk."

Your response could be "I totally understand, which is why I made a quick call to you at work only to get your cell phone number, so we can talk when it's best for you. What time tonight would it be best for us to connect? What number should I call?"

"What exact job do you have in mind and what does it pay?"

Simply explain "I don't have a specific job in mind because your résumé or LinkedIn profile only shows me what you've done and what you're currently doing. What I'm interested in is what you see as your next career move. I don't want to assume that what you're doing now is exactly what you want to do next. When would it be best for us to talk?"

The first time you hear an objection, you may not be able to overcome it. Treat each objection as a learning experience, and use it to help you prepare for how you might overcome the objection the next time. Know that it will take time to learn how to easily overcome objections.

Overcoming objections is a skill you must master, and the only way to improve is to practice. Every time you hear an objection you can't overcome, write it down and role-play with your peers. You will eventually be able to overcome all objections, even seasonal ones like "I'm waiting to receive my holiday bonus" or "I have a vacation planned in two months." You can always negotiate around those objections, and remember, objections are a request for more information, not an obstacle. You will eventually learn to welcome objections.

Summary

You've now learned how identifying the best talent and communicating with them effectively requires a high-tech, high-touch approach. This approach makes you more efficient while developing long-standing relationships with candidates that will benefit you and your hiring authorities not only now, but in the future. You learned where to find talent and how to communicate effectively to engage top talent including looking for nonverbal cues. You also learned to prioritize your candidates' needs and how to relate across multiple generations. You've also learned how to recruit passive candidates and were provided with recruiting scripts and how to effectively overcome candidate objections, which you've learned are requests for more information. The bottom line of this chapter is you will fill more open requisitions because you now know how to communicate with and recruit the best talent.

Key takeaways

- Technology has made it quicker and easier to find candidates who match specific criteria and job requirements.

- Separate the best talent from average candidates by screening for traits of peak performers.

- By adding a high-touch approach to your recruiting efforts, you can identify passive candidates, who represent 85 percent of the current talent pool.

- Build your pipeline of candidates and clients by asking your hiring authorities for candidates or companies they respect.

- Identify passive talent by reaching out to your candidate network for referrals.

- When communicating with hiring authorities and candidates, both parties need to feel heard and understood.

- Ask questions that prioritize your candidates' needs.

- Communicate authoritatively and with confidence.

- Choose your communication tool only after assessing the situation in order to choose the tool that will be most effective.

- You have a moral and ethical responsibility to do the best job you can for every candidate you recruit.

- Overcoming objections is a skill you must master.

Endnotes

1   LinkedIn Talent Solutions, https://business.linkedin.com/talent-solutions (archived at https://perma.cc/V94W-9C9L)
2   "How to Use Twitter to Recruit Top Talent," Akken Cloud, nd, https://www.akkencloud.com/twitterrecruiting (archived at https://perma.cc/4CMJ-ZS2J)

Interview to hire the best talent 3

As recruiters, we conduct so many interviews daily that it's easy to find ourselves asking questions that sound repetitious or even redundant. Yet it's important to remember that the interview is the foundation for the entire hiring process. Interviews provide valuable information about a candidate's credentials, core values, what they consider career advancement, and an individual's potential for success in a specific role. Interviews also provide an opportunity for the candidate to determine if their career goals match up with your company's opportunities and goals.

What is most critical when conducting interviews is ensuring that you are obtaining the information that is most critical to making the best hiring decision. While we all feel the pressure to fill open job requisitions, our success is dependent on our ability to place candidates who will remain in their positions for the long term. The interview process is critical as it is the best opportunity for you to ask questions that will provide you with the information needed to discern which candidates will be a good fit for the company, both in terms of their specific job responsibilities and the overall company culture.

This chapter provides guidance on how to interview so that you successfully identify the best hires who stay on to become engaged employees. Before you begin to interview, it's critical that you know what you are trying to accomplish, which is why I have outlined the five key objectives of an effective interview process. Using those five objectives, you can then begin to conduct interviews. I outline a four-round structured interviewing process to help you evaluate and compare candidates quickly and fairly. By meeting these objectives and following the four-round structured interview process, you can be sure that you are gathering the information that allows your hiring authorities to make the best hiring decision.

Objective 1: Understand the purpose behind the job posting

Have you ever interviewed a candidate who met all the job requirements only to have that same candidate rejected by the hiring manager? Or has a hiring authority ever withdrawn a job requisition without prior notice because of a change in hiring priorities? Finding the best talent in a competitive marketplace is difficult enough. Your job as a recruiter becomes even harder when you aren't aware of the needs and priorities of the hiring authority.

To save yourself time and frustration, take time to understand the reasons that are driving the hiring authority to fill this position before you begin your interview process. Ask the hiring manager why they are currently looking to fill this position. Is this position intended to cover current weaknesses in the department? Is the company looking to hire new talent that attracts other high potentials to the company? Is the hiring manager looking to upgrade a marginal employee? The more you understand what need the organization is trying to meet by posting this job, the more informed your interview questions will be.

When you understand the motivation of the hiring authority, you begin to position yourself as a trusted advisor and will be perceived as an asset. I recall a situation in which I was asked to recruit an Account Manager for a client company. An internal employee had just been promoted from Account Manager to Director of Client Development, and so they were looking to fill the vacated Account Manager role. I spoke with the newly promoted employee to find out what behaviors and practices had made him so successful as an Account Manager. During our conversation, he admitted to me that he had only accepted the promotion to Director of Client Development because he felt it would look bad if he turned down the promotion. After hearing this, I recommended that he speak with his boss and share his feelings about taking on the position of Director of Client Development. After they spoke, the hiring manager allowed the employee to return to his former role as Account Manager, and I was asked to help the company find and interview candidates for the newly posted position of Director of Client Development. Understanding and caring about the needs of my client enabled me to help the organization identify an unknown problem and, as a result, help them fill the right position.

Keep in mind that the purpose behind the job posting can change. Another employee could hand in their two-week notice, the company could lose or win a big contract that directly impacts this potential hire, or they could add on skills needed. It's for this reason that you initially ask the same questions during every subsequent conversation with your hiring authority. That question is "Has anything changed since the last time we talked?" You may not be pleased with the answer, but in order for you to recruit and present candidates they will hire, you must stay informed of any changes.

Objective 2: Learn what is most important to a candidate

Your success as a recruiter is dependent on finding candidates who are likely to become engaged, retained employees. This will only happen if you understand what is most important to your candidate and can introduce them to job opportunities that align with their goals, motivations, and values. And the only way to find out what is most important to a candidate is to ask questions and take the time to listen and understand them.

Fine-tune your listening skills to determine what's most important to each candidate interviewed. Recruiters need to listen differently than most interviewers. Rather than listening to judge, agree, or disagree with your candidate, listen to understand where each candidate is coming from so you can see the world through the candidate's eyes.

Listening in this way will help you figure out which opportunity a candidate would accept without hesitation because it represents their next career move. If you're a third-party recruiter, this helps you determine which one of your clients has the company culture and core values that align with each candidate.

One good indicator of a candidate's values can be discovered by asking them what they like most and least about their current or past jobs and if there is a part of their current or past job that they don't want to do in their next job. Have them outline their current or previous job responsibilities and share the responsibilities they would enjoy building on in their next role and what other things must be there for them to experience career growth.

You can also ask them to explain why they left their past jobs. Be careful how you phrase this question as many candidates, when asked directly, tend to provide the same common responses (overworked, money, didn't enjoy the work or boss, lack of work-life balance, commute too far, etc.) for fear of coming across as negative. One way to get candidates to talk more openly about what they didn't like and what they are looking for in a new opportunity is to frame the question differently. Try asking "If you were your boss, tell me five things you'd change that would make your job more enjoyable." Their answer reveals the real reason they will go through the trauma of a job change.

In the recruiting profession, you consistently help people change jobs. It's easy for us to forget this is a major decision that impacts not only the candidate's life, but also impacts the lives of the people they love. Candidates will often resist change unless there is something they can no longer tolerate and can't resolve at their current job. This answer also helps you key in on positions that don't have the similar issues and represents career growth for your candidate.

If the candidate shares that they left their previous role for monetary reasons, be transparent about the salary range of the positions you're presenting to them. The potential risk here is that they may be interested in talking to you simply in order to get a counteroffer from their existing employer. If you've determined money and advancement are your candidate's primary motivators, suggest they approach their current employer and ask for the next promotion and raise.

That way they don't destroy the trust that currently exists between them and their current employer. If they do not succeed in getting their next promotion and raise, they are more likely to accept an offer you extend and not consider a counteroffer.

However, even if money were their primary motive for leaving, they may also be facing other obstacles in their position that more money or a title change cannot fix. Keep an open dialogue with them quantifying their level of interest on a scale of 1 to 10 throughout the interview process so you don't waste your time on a candidate who isn't serious or motivated to accept a new role.

Another way to learn what is important to a candidate is to ask them about their short- and long-term goals. This will help you gauge how long you can expect them to remain in the role if hired. You may be able to provide them with a challenge that satisfies their short-term goals but are unable to help them achieve their long-term career goals. Your hiring authority will then need to make some decisions about their own hiring objectives, that is, do they hire them knowing they will be engaged and challenged for a short period of time, or do they make some changes internally so they can achieve their long-term goals as well? If they are a stellar candidate, they may decide to employ them anyway, knowing they will move on in a couple of years.

You can learn valuable information by asking candidates what job offers they have turned down and more importantly the reasons why they turned the offers down. If the job you offer is comparable to a position they declined, it is likely the candidate will turn down your offer as well.

Determine specifically what they liked about past jobs they've seriously considered and what was missing that caused them to decline job offers. This helps you fine-tune your efforts on their behalf because you know what must be there for them to accept a job offer without hesitation.

Lastly, during your initial interview, your candidate's answers may be guarded because trust and rapport have not been established. Re-ask pertinent questions throughout your interview process because answers often change as you develop trust and rapport with your candidate. Also, your candidate may have a life-changing experience that could cause their priorities or timing to change. This is why you must continue to pre-close to become aware of any changes in priorities or timing and to quantify their level of interest.

We interviewed a single mom who had turned down three great job offers in Chicago. The jobs all seemed to match what was most important to her, so we continued to probe further. We then uncovered the fact that she wanted to move back home to Indianapolis for several compelling reasons. She wanted her daughters in a great school system and she was attracted by the lower cost of living, but her greatest motivator to move was her mom's failing health. No other recruiter had asked where she preferred to live, which is why she turned down offers in Chicago as her mother's health got worse.

Never assume your candidates want to stay in the same profession or live in the same city, and never think you know what is most important to them. The candidate accepted the first job we presented to her in Indianapolis, without hesitation.

Objective 3: Determine if the candidate is a good fit for your company

In the interview process, performance objectives are the lens through which you can assess whether a candidate will succeed in a specific role. Using these objectives as your guide, review the candidate's work history, and ask questions to help you determine if their achieved goals and objectives are comparable to what they will face in the new opportunity. This will help you screen in candidates who have the best chance of succeeding by achieving the performance objectives of your job. Ask candidates to quantify their confidence (on a scale of 1 to 10) in their ability to meet performance objectives. This will help eliminate the misinterpretation of answers provided and help you in your decision to screen a candidate in or out.

It is also useful to ask the hiring authority for a list of characteristics of engaged employees, ranking each by their level of importance. During the interview, ask candidates to identify their soft and transferable skills and rank their level of expertise on a scale of 1 to 10.

Have them provide an example where they utilized the skills, and ask if their soft or transferable skills are something they want to utilize in their next job. Often potential hires may have the soft or transferable skills your job requires but may not want to utilize them, which is why further clarification is necessary. There are also situations where your candidate has soft or transferable skills they are not using at their current job, which is one of their motivators to change jobs.

Objective 4: Determine if your candidate is a high performer

Too often résumés or CVs or even answers provided during interviews can exaggerate or embellish the truth. The best way to determine if your candidate is truly a high performer is to ask them about their accomplishments and what impact their accomplishments had on past employers. Accomplishments often reveal the candidate's attitude, motivation to attain goals, problem-solving abilities, and work ethic. They can also provide information that may have not been revealed when discussing work history. Uncovering additional soft and transferrable skills will often reveal the type of projects that motivate this candidate. High performers articulate their accomplishments with ease, understand their impact, get promoted often, accept high-level responsibilities, receive honors and incentives, and are often recognized by their employer.

Start out by asking the candidate to discuss their greatest work accomplishment. The answer to this question reveals what they consider to be important. If they share a story about how they helped save the company time and energy, you can assume that they align their own success with the company's success. If, however, a candidate responded, "I finally learned our CRM system and didn't call support every day," you could surmise that this candidate's goals are more personal and perhaps not as aligned with the company's success. The response also indicates that they may struggle with adapting to technology. Neither of these responses would lead you to believe that the candidate is a high performer.

Often when you ask a candidate to list their accomplishments and impact on past employers, they can't think of any. They often don't realize you're not looking for someone who cured cancer but want to know what they've done that made them stand out from past employees who had their job. Ask your candidates if they've ever saved a prior employer time or money, which can be quantified for your hiring authority. These questions help you identify high performers but are also preparing your candidates to present their accomplishments and impact throughout the entire interview process.

Objective 5: Eliminate emotion and bias from the interview process

Everyone has bias. Without realizing it, recruiters can allow their own bias and emotion to impact the interview and hiring process. By not taking steps to prevent emotion and bias from impacting the interviewing process, the interviewer may end up mistaking the best candidate for a lesser candidate who reflects their own bias.

One way to avoid bias or emotion in the interview process is to screen candidates by phone before bringing them in for an in-person interview. Phone screening helps you avoid bias based on a candidate's appearance and allows you to devote your attention to asking questions that will help you determine if the candidate is qualified and a good match with the company culture.

Another way to avoid bias is to have all interviewers use the same criteria to evaluate candidates. This is best accomplished by using an interview scorecard, as in Figure 3.1. During the in-person interviews, all interviewers would use the interview scorecard to rate candidates on a five-point scale in three areas—performance objectives, technical skills, and soft skills.

While it may be impossible to eliminate all bias and emotion from the interview process, conducting the first interview by phone and using the interview scorecard can help to screen in enough qualified candidates to ensure that candidates who move on to the remaining interview rounds (the job audition and the final interview) are the

Figure 3.1 Interview scorecard

INTERVIEW SCORECARD

Candidate name: _____ Date: _____

Position interviewed for: _____

Name of interviewer: _____

Rank the candidate using a scale of 1 to 5 (5 being highest)

Criteria	Interview rating (1–5)	After-hire performance (1–5)	Gap	Action items
Performance objective #1				
Performance objective #2				
Performance objective #3				
Performance objective #4				
Performance objective #5				
Performance objective #6				
Technical ability				
Soft skill examples:				
• Communication				
• Interpersonal/team				
• Organizational				
• Problem solving				

TOTAL:

AVERAGE RATING:

Rating definitions:

5 – Candidate is well versed in this area and will need little or no training
4 – Candidate has done similar work, but minimal experience in this area
3 – Candidate can do the work, but will need training
2 – Candidate lacks this experience or skill
1 – Unqualified

Candidates who average a 3 or less should be eliminated from consideration

Additional interview notes:

Concerns:

most qualified candidates and not reflective of any emotion or bias on the part of the interviewers.

I was contacted by a Fortune 100 company that had launched a major diversity hiring initiative, but it didn't result in diverse hires. They had large government contracts they stood to lose if they did not increase the number of diverse hires. I quickly observed three glaring issues in their hiring process that were sabotaging diverse hiring. First, there were no diverse individuals involved in the hiring process. Second, it took only one person to eliminate a candidate from consideration versus obtaining a group consensus. Lastly, they had not identified new recruiting sources that would attract diverse candidates. They had every intention of hiring diverse candidates but had made no changes to eliminate the bias from their sourcing, interviewing, and hiring process. They addressed these three areas, removing bias from their hiring process, and succeeded in hiring outstanding diverse candidates.

Conducting interviews using the structured four-round interview process

I've had clients extend a job offer after one interview, and I've had other clients conduct eight interviews. However, I recommend what is commonly referred to as the "Rule of Four." After reviewing five years of interviewing data, Google's People Analytics Team found that four interviews were enough to predict whether someone should be hired.[1] I also recommend that all interview rounds be structured to help prevent emotion and bias and to allow for fair and fast evaluation. Next I provide an overview and guide to conducting each of the four rounds of interviews.

Round 1: The telephone screening interview

The telephone screening interview is the foundation for the entire interviewing process. Because this first round of interviews is done by phone, it helps prevent against bias based on personal appearance.

Table 3.1 Telephone screening interview questions

Questions	Answers reveal...
Why are you interested in this job?	Candidate's understanding of your job
Why are you interested in working for our company?	Research conducted
Why are you leaving your current position?	If a situation exists at your company
What qualified you for this position?	Confidence level and credentials
What will be your greatest challenge?	Confidence level and credentials
What is the greatest problem you've solved?	Level of problem-solving skills
What is your greatest accomplishment?	Their priorities
What was the impact of accomplishments on your past employers?	If accomplishments were company focused

A comprehensive telephone interview also helps you determine whether a candidate is qualified and should be recommended for a second interview. The questions you ask at this stage (see Table 3.1) will help you determine a candidate's qualifications for the position, so it is important to ensure that you capture the pertinent information.

Figure 3.2 shows the recommended nine-step telephone interview process comprised of the following stages: prepare, schedule, introduction, interview, follow-up questions, accomplishments and impact, notes, screen in or out, and schedule second interview.

Figure 3.2 Nine-step telephone interview process

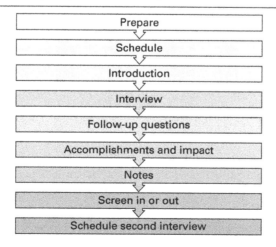

Step 1: Prepare questions in advance

Time is limited, which is why it's important to focus on essential questions that will provide you with the most useful answers. Broad interview questions rarely give you any valuable insight into whether a prospective candidate is a fit for your job or company. Questions should be customized to fit your company's specific hiring needs.

Step 2: Scheduling

The scheduling process should be simple and automated. Set up a 30-minute conversation, but block off additional time on your calendar. Offer to set up a telephone interview before or after working hours, for candidates who are currently employed and not available to openly interview when they are at work.

Step 3. Introduction

Begin with a brief introduction of who you are and a short description of the company. Let candidates know you've been successful helping individuals just like them advance their careers. To further engage the candidate, share some exciting things about the company that the candidate would not have read online. Examples could include a recent acquisition, a new contract approved, an expansion plan, or new training programs being rolled out.

> *"My name is Barb Bruno, and I've been helping individuals like you advance their careers for over 15 years. I'm looking forward to finding out what is most important to you in your next career move."*

> *"It's a very exciting time for our company. We will grow by over 35 percent in the next two years. It's also an exciting time for our employees, because we believe in promoting from within so they can experience career growth."*

Next, give a short description of the opportunity you're attempting to fill. If you're a third-party recruiter, you would share that you have many different opportunities and want to find out what's most important to the candidate before you focus on a specific company or opportunity. Assure the candidate that the purpose of the telephone interview is for both of you to determine if the job you have available is a match and what each candidate sees as their next career move.

> *"We need to hire someone who wants the chance to lead a growing team of hardworking (local) developers and has experience working across many technologies and projects. There is no specific technology/language requirement for this job, but to date most of our projects have been designed for the responsive web. We're looking for someone who may be tired of a mundane cubicle job and wants to join a friendly, passionate team with unlimited potential. The purpose of this interview is for us to determine if this job represents what you see as your next career move."*

Step 4. Ask consistent interview questions

Every candidate should be asked identical questions to ensure consistency and improve your ability to compare candidates. Consistent questioning also helps attain legal compliance and protects from claims of discrimination. If the candidate's responses seem guarded, ask them a few questions to help them feel comfortable talking about themselves. This also gives you a chance to evaluate their communication skills and how they organize their thoughts. This first question also focuses on what's most important to the candidate, so it helps to establish rapport.

> *"To get to know you better, I'd like to know why you've made job changes in the past and what must be there for you to consider a change now."*

People are creatures of habit and will often consider a job change for reasons very similar to the reasons they considered their current job. The only time this is not accurate is when a candidate has had a major life event like a marriage, divorce, birth of a child, death, or relocation. These events can change the reasons why a candidate will consider a change.

Next, inform the candidate that you have reviewed their résumé or CV, and then ask about current projects. Most résumés and LinkedIn profiles are not kept up to date, and work they've recently done could impact your decision.

"I've reviewed your résumé and would love to know a little more about you. What are some of the latest projects you've been involved with?"

You would then ask the list of questions you created for each position. I've listed some possible questions for in-house recruiters below.

"Why are you interested in this job?"

"Why are you interested in working for our company?"

"What qualifies you for this position?"

Step 5. Ask follow-up questions

If you don't understand a candidate's response to your question, ask follow-up questions so you can obtain clarification. Confirm your candidate's definition of words used. Your candidates will appreciate that you care enough not only to listen to their responses, but to also clarify your understanding of what they are saying. Rather than asking about a candidate's current salary, which is now illegal due to salary ban laws in many states in the US, you could verify what salary range they are seeking to make sure this candidate's expectations fall within your hiring budget.

Step 6. Ask about accomplishments and impact

These are the most important questions during every step of your recruiting and interview process. What separates good from great candidates are the accomplishments they've achieved and the impact they had on past employers. Their answers also reveal their priorities and what they're most proud of, which is great insight into every candidate.

Try asking:

"What is the greatest problem you've solved?"

"What is your greatest accomplishment and what was the impact?"

Hiring authorities will assume this candidate will achieve similar accomplishments that will also provide a positive impact.

Step 7. Enter notes

Enter your notes into your ATS or CRM system, making information easily accessible to everyone involved in the hiring process. This is especially important because you will conduct interviews daily for different job opportunities. After several days of interviewing, it can be difficult remembering which candidates stood out for specific requisitions.

Step 8. Decide to screen in or out

At the end of the phone interview process, compare all candidates and determine who you screen in or out. The clear signs that candidates won't work out include low energy, too much focus on money, their LinkedIn profile and résumé don't match, or they're unsure of the job they will accept. Provide feedback to all of the candidates you interview to make sure everyone has a positive experience, whether they are set up with a second interview or screened out. This prevents negative posts on social media, results in referrals of great talent, and provides information to candidates screened out that can help improve their job search. Trust your instincts and don't forward a candidate who doesn't feel right.

Step 9. Schedule second interview

The purpose of the phone interview is to screen candidates over the phone instead of an in-person interview. This saves you time, streamlines your hiring process, and will help you fine-tune your recruiting efforts. You then screen out unqualified candidates and schedule the best candidates for a second interview. I strongly recommend a panel interview in the interest of having an efficient interview process, so you can attract and hire the best candidates.

Round 2: The panel interview

Panel interviews should be limited to no more than four people. One person is assigned as the leader while other panel members play supporting roles. The hiring manager and at least two other individuals involved in the hiring decision should participate on the panel.

Table 3.2 Responsibilities of panel interviewers

The panel leader	Other panel members
Asks prepared questions focused on the performance objectives	Ask follow-up questions to clarify questions
Asks about accomplishments	Ask follow-up questions about impact of accomplishments
Asks questions to determine characteristics and core values	Clarify answers

Individuals who are selected as panel members should either directly or indirectly interact with the prospective candidate if hired. All panel members should prepare in advance by reading the job requisition and understanding the performance objectives as well as the characteristics and culture of the department. See Table 3.2 for responsibilities of panel interviewers.

Allow at least 90 minutes for the panel interview. The hiring manager or leader of the panel should focus on questions that reveal if the candidate could perform successfully on the job, their past patterns of success, accomplishments, and reasons for career moves. Other panel members should ask clarifying questions that are assigned in advance that delve deeper into whether the candidate will be successful on the job. These could include abilities like technical competency, motivation, planning, problem solving, and the candidate's character.

Measure candidate responses against the performance objectives using the 1–5 rating system.

After the interview, panel members meet to review their interviewing notes and scorecards to determine if the candidate is screened in or out of consideration.

Round 3: The job audition

If screened in, the candidate should be scheduled for the job audition, in which the candidate experiences a day "on the job" at your company. During the job audition, the potential hire is experiencing your company, culture, and peers firsthand. Watching a job in action will either increase or decrease a candidate's level of interest. When interviewing prospective recruiters at my company, we taught them how to make recruiting calls, gave them a script, and role-played overcoming objections. We provided them with a list of prospective candidates to hire. We also explained that if they were successful in having someone send them a résumé and we ended up hiring or placing that candidate, we would pay them a $500 bonus. This step in the interview process is an actual job audition. The potential hire is experiencing your company, culture, and peers firsthand while they audition for your job.

We also found that the job audition is a great means of identifying someone who is a great fit or, conversely, detecting red flags. In my company, red flags included phone fear, disruptive personality, inability to overcome any objections, too talkative, lack of listening skills, or being very opinionated. While these traits were difficult to detect in the telephone or panel interview, they were quickly identified by peers who were observing them during their audition. (Involving their peers in the job audition also resulted in their buy-in when we decided which candidate was to be hired.)

Ultimately, the job audition helped us avoid making bad hires and improved the engagement and retention of candidates who performed well during their job audition.

Stage 4: The final interview

Candidates who reach the final interview stage are those whom interviewers believe could successfully meet the performance objectives. Reference checks, assessments, and background checks have all been satisfactorily completed, and candidate scorecards have been reviewed.

The final interview is conducted by the hiring manager. During this interview the candidate is asked to clarify any areas of concerns, while the hiring manager makes their final assessment of the candidate's alignment with the company culture, core values, department, and current team members. It's important to listen intently to questions being asked by the candidate because their questions often reveal their priorities or concerns. This is the last chance in the interviewing process to address any red flags or concerns because you don't want to extend a job offer that will be rejected. Secondly, it's the last time you can explain how the priorities of the candidate align with the priorities of your hiring authorities. Lastly, in this candidate-driven market and with the accessibility of other job opportunities utilizing technology, this is the last opportunity you have to also quantify the candidate's level of interest in your job as opposed to other opportunities they may be considering

If the final interview is successful, a compensation package is compiled, and the job offer is extended to the candidate. For mid- to upper-level positions, consider extending the offer over lunch or dinner to eliminate all distractions and affirm the importance and excitement of welcoming them to your existing team. It's important to ask your candidate for the name of their favorite restaurant or type of cuisine they prefer, to avoid possible food allergies. I once had an employer invite a candidate to the best sushi restaurant in Chicago, and my candidate did not eat sushi. After I explained this to our hiring authority, the dinner was switched to a steak house. Focusing on the cuisine most enjoyed by your candidate also sends a subtle message that you focus on little things that your employees enjoy and prefer.

Summary

The interview is the foundation for the entire hiring process. However, you are also judged if the candidates you place become engaged and retained employees. This chapter outlined the importance of clarifying the five key objectives of an effective interview before you begin to interview. You were then shown the advantages of a four-round structured interview process to help you gather the information that allows your hiring authorities to make the best hiring decisions.

You also understand how priorities and timing can change throughout the interview process. In addition, you now realize the impact technology has on a candidate's ability to reach out to their network and interview for other job opportunities. For these reasons, you've learned how to pre-close, re-interview, and continue to quantify interest. Lastly, you learned why it's important to make a lasting impression when an offer is extended.

Key takeaways

- Understand what is driving the hiring authority to fill a position before you begin to interview.

- When you understand the motivation of your hiring authority, you position yourself as a more valuable asset.

- The purpose behind the job posting can change.

- Always ask your hiring authorities "Has anything changed since the last time we talked?"

- If you want your candidates to become engaged and retained employees, you need to determine what is most important to each candidate.

- Prepare your questions in advance, knowing what you want the answer to reveal about each candidate and to ensure consistency during your interviews.

- Listen to understand the values, goals, and motivations of your candidate so you can make better matches.

- Never judge, agree, or disagree with your candidates; listen to understand where they're coming from.

- If you're a third-party recruiter, determine which client had the opportunity, company culture, and core values that would be the best match for each candidate.

- To determine a candidate's values, ask them what they liked most and least about past jobs.

- To determine why a candidate will consider another opportunity, ask this question: "If you were your boss, tell me five things you would change to make your job more enjoyable."

- Be wary of candidates who are simply looking for an increase in salary. They could be using you to obtain a counteroffer from their current employer.

- Understand what offers your candidate has received and turned down and why they turned the offers down.

- During an initial interview, answers are guarded because trust and rapport have not been established.

- Re-ask pertinent questions and pre-close candidates to determine if any changes have occurred.

- Retention can be accurately predicted when you uncover a candidate's short-term as well as long-term goals.

- Identify accomplishments and the impact they had on past employers.

- Performance objectives determine if your candidate can succeed in a specific role.

- Peak performers are revealed by the impact their accomplishments had on past employers, their track record of success, and recognition they've received throughout their career.

- The four-round structured interview process helps prevent emotion and bias from affecting hiring decisions by ensuring that all candidates are asked the same questions and evaluated fairly.

- Make recommendations to streamline the interview process to attract the best talent for your hiring authorities. A comprehensive telephone interview also helps you determine whether a candidate is qualified and should be recommended for a second interview. I recommend a nine-step telephone interview process comprised of the following stages: prepare, schedule, introduction, interview, follow-up questions, accomplishments and impact, notes, screen in or out, and schedule second interview.

- Phone interviews are designed to help you screen candidates in or out. The clear signs during a phone interview that candidates won't work out include low energy, too much focus on money, their LinkedIn profile and résumé don't match, or they're unsure of the job they will accept.

- It's important that every candidate have a positive experience to avoid negative posts on social media. Every candidate should be asked identical questions to ensure consistency and improve your ability to compare candidates. Consistent questioning also helps attain legal compliance and protects from claims of discrimination.

- The job audition is a great means of identifying candidates who represent either a great culture fit or, conversely, exhibit red flags. Culture fit or red flags may be difficult to detect in the telephone or panel interview but are more easily identified during the job audition.

Endnote

1   Michael Schneider, "Google Can Predict Whether You'll Get Hired After 4 Interviews," *Inc.*, nd, https://www.inc.com/michael-schneider/5-years-of-google-data-reveals-number-of-interviews-it-takes-to-find-perfect-candidate.html (archived at https://perma.cc/V94W-9C9L)

Clarify timing with hiring authorities and candidates

4

Timing impacts your personal and professional life, just as it has a tremendous impact on the recruiting process. It's always very satisfying when everything falls in place, but unexpected things often happen in life that then impact the timing of candidates or clients involved in your hiring process.

Instead of thinking of yourself as a recruiter, imagine for a moment that you're the conductor of a symphony orchestra. Every musician in the orchestra will follow your lead for timing, as songs slow down or speed up according to the score of music. If one musician's timing is off, it impacts the entire orchestra and will flaw a perfect performance. In recruiting, the score of music is your open requisition, and everyone involved in the hiring process and your candidate are the orchestra. It's your job to stay aware of the timing, in order to end up filling your requisition with the best hire and achieve a perfect performance.

Life's unforeseen circumstances can cause timing delays, and they are not that uncommon when individuals are juggling their professional and personal lives. When I was a single mom, I was constantly trying to balance the conflicting priorities of my family and business. I vividly remember panicking when my daughter spiked a fever the night before our best client was scheduled to conduct final interviews for three candidates in my office. I remember scrambling the next morning to find someone who could take care of her until my interviews were completed.

Throughout my more than 20 years of recruiting experience, I've realized that our process is reliant on great sourcing, an efficient interview process, planning, hard work, and most importantly, perfect timing. It's critical that the target date to hire of your hiring authority and the preferred timing of your candidate to accept a new opportunity align, but take into consideration that their priorities and timing often change. It's for this reason you need to consistently confirm your understanding of preferred timing with both your candidates and hiring authorities.

This chapter addresses the importance of timing in the recruiting process—specifically how your efforts as a recruiter are affected by the timing obstacles of a competitive job market. We also address how requisitions, the hiring process, and demands impact timing. Next, we will outline what hiring authority timing issues you can control and which timing obstacles are out of your control.

This chapter will then focus on how timing impacts your interactions with your candidates as we reveal the possible inefficiencies of your online application process and how technology impacts the timing of candidates. Lastly, this chapter shows you how to anticipate other timing obstacles.

Timing obstacles of a competitive job market

Think of the frustration of recruiting, interviewing, and presenting the perfect candidate for one of your challenging requisitions, only to have your candidate cancel their interview due to a conflict in their schedule. Also think of the times you had a candidate accept an offer only to call you a few days before their start date to tell you they've changed their mind because their company just announced a significant bonus program, or they decided to accept a counteroffer. Then there are candidates who start their new job, leave for lunch, and never return without any explanation. Or the most dreaded call a recruiter can receive: "Where is your candidate, I thought they were starting today?" This is especially frustrating when you had talked to your candidate the evening before their start date to wish them good luck, and there was no indication they didn't plan to show up on their first day of employment.

In this competitive job market, the examples I listed dramatically impact timing and happen far too frequently. The best candidates are regularly being contacted by multiple recruiters. As a result they are choosing from among multiple opportunities and don't necessarily stop interviewing, or even hand in their two-week notice, after they've accepted your job offer. In fact, candidates will often request an extended notice because they want to see if they receive other offers.

Too often hiring authorities realize there is a competitive job market but have not shortened their hiring process, which causes you to lose top talent due to timing. Job offers that allow candidates to split their time between working virtually and working on-site are also very desirable. Companies that are not offering flexible work schedules to potential hires are also losing out on hiring great talent.

Hiring authorities and timing

Whether you are in a face-to-face intake session with a hiring authority or obtaining specs over the phone, there are things you can do to influence the time frame of your hiring authorities. When you obtain a new requisition, first ask what resources they've already utilized so you don't waste your valuable time duplicating prior recruiting efforts. Your hiring authorities do not want you to present the same candidates they've surfaced from website postings and job board ads. They want you to recruit passive candidates, who represent 85 percent of the talent pool.

Hiring authorities are not going to extend their target date to fill or hire an average candidate because your recruiting efforts are not surfacing the caliber of talent they prefer to hire. They expect you to recruit candidates who become engaged and retained employees while you meet their target date to hire.

You will have several interactions with hiring authorities that impact timing and either enhance or sabotage your ability to recruit and present the best talent to your hiring authorities. The information you obtain during your intake session is the foundation for your entire recruiting process. To conduct a successful recruiting process, understand the impact of timing, request a specific target date to hire, and three interview times. When you are merely told the job needs to be filled ASAP or immediately, you don't know when to begin your recruiting efforts or if the individuals involved in the hiring process are available to interview.

For example: One of our clients called us after Thanksgiving and gave us an exclusive search for a VP of HR, and the target start date was before the end of the year. They wanted this hire to be included in the current year's hiring budget. The hiring process for this company was five weeks, due to their background and assessment checks and their four-interview process.

I immediately asked my client if we could scale the interview process down to a panel and final interview, which he agreed to. He also agreed to conduct the background checks and assessments immediately following the panel interview. He also understood that we could only present candidates who were unemployed, because there was not enough time for an employed candidate to hand in a two-week notice. I asked him to get back to me with a date for the panel interview, and he called back with a date for the panel interview of January 5.

My first question was about their desire to have this person start before the end of the year. He explained the individuals who would participate on the panel interview were not available until after the first of the year, and later got back to me with a start date of February 1.

Had we not determined the availability of the individuals in the hiring process, this would have been a top-priority recruit that would have wasted our time. We could now present candidates who were employed and had more time to conduct a thorough recruit. If we had worked on the recruit in November, we would have lost the candidates because the hiring process would have taken too long. This is just one example of how important it is for you to clarify timing, both the target date to hire and if people involved in the hiring process are available to interview.

Also, when you obtain a specific target date to fill specific requisitions, you can better estimate when to begin recruiting. For example, you should allocate more time for positions that require skills that are hard to find or for higher-level positions that may involve a nationwide or international search, which involves a longer, more intensive interviewing process. Be careful not to start too early, as it may be too far ahead to schedule interviews, and candidates are not likely to wait around if the process does not keep moving forward. You also can't start too late or you may not be able to surface talent by the target date.

Next, when you review the hiring process, if the process involves more than four interviews, share the benefit of limiting the interview process to four. This also helps you elevate your relationship with your hiring managers by positioning yourself as a workforce/workplace expert. Suggest a panel interview to combine multiple interviews and shorten the time to hire. Work with the hiring authority to confirm who will participate in the process, and obtain the times they are available for interviews. You need to confirm that everyone who needs to interview the candidate has a chance to meet them and that there is enough time for the interviewers to reach their decision by the target date to hire as well as the preferred time frame of the candidate.

Timing is also impacted when specifications of a job requisition change after interviews are conducted. This often happens when requisitions are not updated or the candidate's direct report is looking for skills not included. This can tremendously delay the hiring decision, which can throw off timing for both your hiring authority and candidate. To resolve this, email a copy of the job requisition to everyone involved in the hiring process. As we discussed in Chapter 1, getting the input on the job requisition before you begin the interview process will ensure that everyone agrees with the scope, skills, and performance objectives that the position requires. You will be amazed at how much more quickly the process goes when you receive input on the job requisition before you begin the interviewing process.

Take time to understand the cost of this unfilled position to the hiring authority. If there is no problem and another employee is covering the job, the hiring authority may delay filling the job to save money.

This affects the timing of your recruiting efforts because there is no urgency to fill the job. However, if they face a situation where there is no coverage for this position and the open requisition is costing the company money, or if the employee covering the job is threatening to quit because of the added workload, this is a priority search.

If you are given a purple squirrel search or a very demanding requisition, explain why the opportunity will take much longer to fill if you are able to recruit the talent requested. Provide Friday updates explaining the lack of talent to present and share the details of your search efforts. Your feedback can encourage hiring authorities to makes changes so that you are recruiting on a requisition you can more than likely fill by the agreed-upon target date.

Technology has had a tremendous impact on the recruiting profession and definitely impacts timing of both your hiring managers and candidates. Your hiring managers understand that you utilize technology to help identify talent, and as a result they expect you to surface top talent faster. It's up to you to manage their expectations of the time you need to recruit the best talent. Technology certainly impacts the speed at which you find and attract the best candidate, but it's important to recognize that it is a tool and not the solution.

Prospective candidates have also learned to hide behind technology. When is the last time you called a prospective candidate and they answered their phone? It's easy for candidates to hide behind voicemail, email, and InMail. Unfortunately, it's easy for a candidate to ignore these forms of communication. When I've addressed technology conferences, hard-to-find IT talent shared that they receive as many as 20 to 30 InMail a week from recruiters. They often feel these are a waste of their time, so they decide to ignore them.

While technology helps you screen and present candidates faster, it is also true that most recruiters use the same technology and social media outlets to post jobs, recruit and screen candidates, and track their candidates internally. As a result, the best talent is bombarded with email, InMail, and the number of opportunities being presented. As a result, they will weigh your position against all the others, making your job more difficult.

If your hiring managers are willing to utilize technology like Skype to conduct initial interviews, technology will help escalate the timing of the hiring process. However, you can't simply depend on technology and expect to be successful in filling your job requisitions faster with the best talent. Your competitive advantage comes from your high-touch approach, while continuing to verify the time frame of your hiring authority and candidate. To make sure that you stay informed of any changes in priorities or timing for an open position, during every conversation ask, "Has anything changed since the last time we talked?" This will help you anticipate timing issues that could delay your ability to fill their open requisitions.

While no one can control the multitude of issues that affect timing, there are ways to hedge against unfortunate timing having a negative influence on your hiring process. Try asking yourself these questions: Is this the right time to hire someone? Is your company set up to attract, then support and onboard a new hire? Are you willing to devote the necessary time to attract, interview, vet, and make an attractive offer to a candidate who may be looking at multiple opportunities? Have you gone beyond a typical job description and visualized what your ideal candidate looks like: where they will come from, why they would consider an opportunity with your firm, and how you and your team will support them when they are hired? Have you created a process that allows you to quickly and effectively evaluate your candidates?

If you find someone you're interested in and know you want to move forward with the offer, quickly put them through the process you've established and reach a decision. Depending on your hiring process, the time frame for candidate evaluation will vary, but it's important to be consistent and make decisions quickly, especially when you are attempting to attract hard-to-find candidates. Once you've made a hiring decision, extend the offer. Waiting for a better candidate is never a good idea. If the time is right and everything has been done internally and during the interview process, pre-close your candidate one last time and then extend the offer.

There are also situations that impact timing that are out of your control. Imagine after months of conversations, you finally successfully recruit an executive you targeted from one of your top competitors who expressed interest in working for your company. After enthusiastically presenting this person, you're told by company leadership that even though they would normally jump at the opportunity to hire this executive, timing is not right because of unexpected internal and budget issues.

When budgets are withdrawn, your recruiting efforts come to a screaming halt, even if you have recruited someone you know would greatly benefit the company. There is no way you can anticipate unexpected internal or budget issues. In this instance, you could explain to your candidate that your company continues to have a very high level of interest in talking, but it would benefit them more if these conversations took place in a few months. If you explain how a delay in timing can benefit your candidate and continue to nurture them, they will often agree to your new time frame because they are currently employed and not conducting an active job search.

Candidates and timing

Your ability to fill a position quickly is impacted by the availability and time constraints of your candidates. Because the best candidates will likely be approached by multiple recruiters with different offers, you want to establish a rapport with these candidates as soon as possible. Once you find a promising candidate online, try to schedule a phone call in order to take the conversation offline as quickly as possible. If you can get them on the phone, you can use the communication skills you learned in Chapter 3 to establish rapport and trust. Many candidates can't talk openly if they are working and are not comfortable discussing another job during working hours, so find out when it is convenient for them to talk with you. Then make yourself available even if it means scheduling an appointment during weekends or evenings. When you work around a candidate's schedule, you show them you care, which helps develop rapport and trust.

When you speak with candidates on the phone, share how you have helped other individuals with similar experience advance their careers. Most people are interested in advancing their career, whether they are currently employed or conducting an active job search.

If you are representing a candidate who is currently employed, determine why they are looking, if they are willing to schedule time off to interview, and then obtain a target date from them to change their job.

When a candidate applies to one of your job postings, the process must be short and simple. In order to determine the experience of your candidates, take time to apply to one of your current job postings. If it takes you longer than 15 minutes to apply, streamline your online application process so that you don't lose candidates. Make it easy to apply to your company and be willing to initially accept a LinkedIn profile in lieu of a résumé or CV. Additional information, assessments, or checks required can be obtained later. If your application process takes too long because of online assessments, background, criminal, or credit checks, or other types of verifications, be mindful these delays could cause you to lose highly qualified candidates. The only candidates who can take the time to complete a long application process are candidates who are not working, which is a very limited talent pool with low unemployment rates.

As a recruiter, the initial application and screening is likely the only part of the recruiting process where you are in complete control and can establish the timing. Your ability to quickly screen and hire is primarily dependent on the needs and interests of the hiring authority whose position you are trying to fill as well as the needs and interests of the candidate, who may or may not be interested in the position. Aligning the needs and interests of both parties can be challenging, but effective communication and a firm understanding of your hiring authority's interviewing process and compensation and benefits packages can go a long way toward reducing your time to hire.

Ask other questions that help you determine timing like: "Are you close to becoming vested in your pension fund?" "Do you have any bonuses or incentives that will be paid out in the next six months?" "Do you have any vacation time planned?" You can always negotiate time off without pay unless the candidate has an extended vacation planned shortly after starting. The answers to these questions save time for you, your hiring managers, and the candidates you represent.

When you're representing a candidate who is not working, don't assume that they're open to interview at any time or are available to start immediately. Often candidates who are unemployed accept part-time jobs, accept temporary or contract opportunities, make commitments to friends and family members, draw unemployment benefits, or work on other projects that might delay their decision to accept a job.

Also inquire if the unemployed candidate is conducting their own active job search, has other interviews already scheduled, or is waiting on job offers they've found on their own. They may not want to volunteer this information for fear of alienating you, so use your high-touch communication skills to establish trust and rapport with them. Pick up the phone and have a conversation with them. Explain that you don't want to duplicate any of their efforts or submit their résumé to anyone they have already contacted. You can also inform them that your ability to uncover new opportunities is enhanced if you know what they liked and disliked about companies or opportunities to which they have applied.

Whether candidates are employed or not, you need to keep in close contact with them and make sure they inform you of other interview activities. You don't want to spend time finding opportunities for a candidate who has just accepted another offer. Again, this is why it is critically important to establish rapport and trust with your candidate. When you ask them, "Has anything changed since the last time we talked?," they are more likely to answer you honestly and candidly if they feel they can trust you. As a result, you stay informed and are less likely to be caught off guard if "life happens" and their target date changes.

And believe me, life happens even in those situations where you are sure you have the perfect opportunity for the perfect candidate. I once represented a woman who was looking for a job to supplement her husband's income. Because her husband was the primary income provider, she wasn't looking to work long hours or seeking a demanding career. She simply wanted to find a low-stress job. The day I obtained a job offer for her, I was certain she would accept it without hesitation. Unfortunately, that was the same day her husband asked her for a divorce and moved out. As a result of these changes in her life situation, she decided there was too much turmoil in her life to make a job change. Her job search was put on hold indefinitely.

While you always want to keep informed of your candidate's activities, it's also important to keep candidates informed of any delays or changes in the hiring process. If there are delays, reach out to them and proactively explain the reason for delays. Candidates often see delays as a sign they will be rejected, and they lose interest in the job. Whenever possible, be specific about the reason for the delay so your candidate doesn't assume the worst. Your candidates realize that unexpected delays can happen. By keeping them informed, you fortify their trust in you and hopefully retain them as a candidate for the position.

When the time comes to extend a job offer, confirm that your candidate's time frame aligns with your hiring authority's target date to hire. Beware of candidates who ask if they can give an extended notice to their current employer. An extended notice could indicate that this candidate is actively interviewing or considering other opportunities. Unless you are representing a candidate who will relocate for their new job, the average notice given is two weeks. Throughout your process continue to pre-close your candidate's timing by asking: "If I were to get you an offer at the salary range we discussed, are you ready to hand in your two-week notice today?" If your candidate responds anything but yes, delve deeper to understand what has changed.

While the timing of your hiring authority and candidate present the most common challenges, offers may be delayed or rejected because of restrictions on benefits, bonuses/incentive pay, or even pensions. Let's begin with benefits offered. A job offer is not just a starting salary and date—it includes a benefit plan as well. Make sure you understand the benefit package before you begin your recruiting efforts. It's not enough to understand what benefits are being offered. You need to know when your candidates will be eligible, if they offer single or family coverage, what are the deductibles, whether your candidate pays any of the costs, and whether they can keep their current doctors. You should also understand the difference between the various types of benefit plans.

If you are a third-party recruiter, you should have a copy of the benefits package for every client you represent. Make sure to ask for an updated copy at least once a year, because benefit coverage often changes. Many companies offer benefits with a much higher deductible in an attempt to keep their costs down. If your candidate currently pays low deductibles, this could cause them to reject your offer. A candidate's current benefits and costs must be clarified early in your interview process.

An employed candidate may also defer accepting a job if they have a bonus or incentive pay due to them by their current employer. I had one candidate delay accepting an offer until after their holiday bonus. The hiring authority was not willing to wait and made an offer to a different candidate.

Many companies use pension funds as a retention strategy. Funds vary greatly from one company to another, but let's say, for example, that your candidate will be vested in their pension fund in five years. They are currently five months shy of becoming vested. In this instance, it is in the best interest of the candidate to stay at their current job for the five months, become vested, and then make a job change. Always ask candidates if they have a pension fund and if so, when it will vest. This prevents you from representing a candidate who will interview with you and your hiring authorities, express a high level of interest, but then decline an offer because they want to delay changing their job until they are fully vested.

Anticipate other timing obstacles

Timing, when viewed from a hiring perspective, is important for many reasons. When a company is trying to improve its team by bringing in new talent, it needs to find a strong candidate and wait accordingly. Then, hopefully, everything will fall into place for a successful hire. Sometimes that candidate is simply not available; other times they may be. It's all about timing!

In this candidate-driven job market, waiting too long can push your candidate into the arms of your competition—multiple offers and counteroffers, even for passive candidates, are now the norm. On the other hand, if you act too quickly, you might rush your candidate into making a decision before they have the time they need to truly evaluate your company and the opportunity. If you don't give them enough time to be confident in their decision, they may feel rushed, not take it seriously, turn it down, or even take a counteroffer.

Similarly, you need enough time to properly evaluate your candidate. Otherwise, you may potentially make a bad hire who ends up becoming a costly turnover statistic. Continually evaluate your hiring process and the results you are achieving. Review if the process is structured, consistent, and if all decision-makers are engaged and available to keep the process moving forward. If you're a third-party recruiter, you have the added challenge of reviewing the interview process for multiple companies and clients. However, when you make suggestions that result in successfully hiring the best talent, you also elevate the relationships you have with your clients. They now see how it benefits them to be aware of timing and the impact it has on their hiring process.

For a candidate to confirm they're accepting an opportunity that's right for them, they need to understand the big picture, including any problems they will likely face. The hiring authority may give them a deadline to accept an offer, but the important part of their process is evaluating the opportunity, its pros and cons, and the company culture. If a candidate feels pressured to make their decision or does not have adequate information, too often this results in an offer turn-down. Remember, the hiring process has its own rhythm, but it is continually impacted by the timing of your hiring managers and candidates.

There are other timing obstacles that impact the timing of your hiring authorities and candidates. Natural disasters, such as floods, hurricanes, tornadoes, earthquakes, tsunamis, or volcanic eruptions, can cause a loss of life, damage property, or cause economic damage.

The severity of how natural disasters affect timing depend on the affected population and their resilience.

A vivid example of economic damage and its impact on timing of hiring are the 2020 bushfires that devastated Australia's eastern seaboard, which exceeded the record $4.4 billion set by the Black Saturday blazes in 2009, according to Moody's Analytics. The increased air pollution caused direct harm to industries such as farming and tourism, but also crippled Australia's consumer confidence and damaged the broader economy outside areas ravaged by fire. Can you imagine the impact on hiring in Puerto Rico when it was struck by magnitude 6.4 earthquake in January of 2020, while still suffering economic losses from Hurricane Maria in 2017? I remember having to reschedule the training I was providing for an offshore recruiting team located in Manila because of a typhoon. Natural disasters cause hiring to take a backseat to the immediate actions needed to deal with the disaster, unless the new hires will help a company recover.

Other obstacles to hiring are announcement of a merger, relocation, sale of a company, or major changes in the leadership of a company. The minute you hear these announcements, immediately meet with your hiring managers to determine if the opportunity will be put on hold or if they want you to proceed. Immediately inform pending candidates of the change in timing to determine if they are willing to wait or want to be taken out of consideration.

Lastly, due to the times we live in, it's important to anticipate how terrorism impacts the economy and the timing of your hiring authorities and candidates. The human cost is always devastating, and the economic impact can be substantial. Unfortunately, businesses globally have dealt with the realities and tragedies of global terrorism, and the threat has only increased. These terrorist acts can cause a ripple negative impact on the global economy. They cause a direct economic destruction of property and lives and create market uncertainty, loss of tourism, and increased insurance claims. These events create an influx for certain professions like construction and insurance adjusters but cause most current job opportunities to be put on hold. You need to get in front of these situations and provide people with answers and realistic expectations.

Summary

Chapter 4 has proven how timing has a direct impact on the level of success you will enjoy in the recruiting profession. One of the greatest challenges in recruiting is the fact that you have people on both sides of your process. Unexpected things often happen in life that impact timing. Your candidate could be the peak performer your hiring authority needs, and the opportunity you are presenting could clearly represent career and financial advancement for you candidate. However, if timing is not right for either your hiring manager or candidate, even though you've done your job and made the perfect match, this will not end up as a hire.

We also addressed the timing obstacles that exist as a result of the competitive job market. Globally, there is increased competition for top talent, and candidates will often look at numerous opportunities before accepting an offer. The chapter provided examples of challenges that are on the rise, including the fact that candidates will often accept your offer and continue to interview.

This chapter addresses the importance of shortening the hiring process while also showing the advantage to your hiring managers of offering flexible working options to candidates in order to compete for top talent. You've learned things you can control to expedite the hiring process and how your interactions with hiring authorities can either enhance or sabotage timing and your ability to successfully fill open requisitions.

You have also learned why it's so important to obtain a specific date to hire and interview times, so you know when to begin your sourcing and recruiting efforts. When you review the interview process and determine it's more than a four-step process, you now know how to explain the benefits of a four-interview process, so you don't lose the best talent due to timing. You've also learned how to revise specs for purple squirrel positions, so you can successfully recruit talent to fill those requisitions. You also understand situations you can't control regarding the timing of your hiring authorities.

This chapter then addressed how timing impacts the candidates you recruit. You've learned the importance of a short online application and screening process that won't eliminate the best talent. Questions were provided that can help you determine the timing of your candidates, whether they are working passive candidates or candidates who are not working.

You learned how to extend job offers with an emphasis on benefits, and you learned how to uncover issues that could delay acceptance of your offers. You also now understand the importance of consistently keeping in touch and nurturing your candidates during their two-week notice and after they have started. You also learned questions to ask to make sure you don't invest your valuable time on candidates who are not going to accept an offer.

Lastly, this chapter addressed other timing obstacles, including trying to force candidates to accept a job, natural disasters, mergers, relocation, major changes in leadership, or, sadly, terrorist events that impact the economy and job market. When you proactively are aware of the impact of timing throughout your recruiting efforts, utilize technology, and anticipate changes, timing will work in your favor and you will fill more requisitions.

Key takeaways

- Timing is affected by the obstacles of the competitive global job market.
- Life's unforeseen circumstances can cause timing delays.
- Delays are common as candidate juggle their professional and personal lives.
- It's critical that the target date to hire aligns with your candidate's timing to accept a job.
- Candidates are in demand and are being contacted by multiple recruiters.
- Too often hiring authorities have not shortened their hiring process to hire top talent.
- The intake session is the foundation for your recruiting process and affects timing.

- Your interactions with clients impact timing and either enhance or sabotage your efforts.

- Obtaining a target date to fill and interview times help determine priority searches.

- Limit the hiring process to four interviews.

- Send a copy of your requisition to everyone up front to avoid changes after you've presented qualified candidates.

- Learn the cost of the unfilled position and problems that exist to determine urgency to hire.

- Technology has changed recruiting and does impact the speed at which you can identify candidates, but it's a tool, not a solution.

- Your high-tech and high-touch recruiting efforts will provide you with a competitive edge.

- Your online application process must be short and simple, or you will lose top talent.

- To avoid duplication, clarify what efforts your client has made to fill their requisition.

- Clarify the availability and time constraints of your candidates.

- Ask questions about candidates' existing benefits to determine if any obstacle like a vested pension fund would change their time frame.

- Keep informed of your candidate's other interview activity.

- Start every conversation with candidates and clients with "Has anything changed since the last time we talked?"

- Confirm that your candidate's time frame aligns with your hiring authority's target date to hire.

- Clarify your candidate's timing and interest throughout your interviewing process by asking them "If I were to get you an offer in the salary range we discussed, are you ready to hand in your two-week notice today?"

- Keep candidates informed of delays in your hiring process, or you will lose them.

- Know the details on the current benefits of your candidate and benefits you are offering to avoid extending an offer that won't be accepted due to benefits.

- Third-party recruiters should request a current copy of the benefits package for every client.

- It's important to anticipate other timing obstacles.

- Waiting too long to extend an offer can result in your losing the candidate.

- Anticipate changes in timing due to natural disasters.

- Anticipate changes in timing due to mergers, relocation, sales of a company, or major changes in the leadership of a company.

- Lastly, anticipate how terrorism impacts the economy and timing of hiring authorities and candidates.

Extend offers that will be accepted

5

Obtaining a job offer for a recruited candidate should be your reward for a job well done, but unfortunately, a recruiter's work doesn't end there. According to one survey, 28 percent of candidates backed out after receiving a job offer because they accepted a better offer; 44 percent accepted a counteroffer from their current employer; 27 percent heard bad things about the company; 19 percent felt the job didn't have growth potential.[1]

While you can't control the behavior of your hiring authorities or candidates, you can prepare yourself to face challenges that may arise when extending an offer. The most effective way I've found to prevent offers from being declined is to understand all the factors that may affect a candidate's decision to accept or reject a position. I can then create a strategy to effectively respond to them.

Why candidates turn down offers

During the Q & A portion of the weekly job search webinars I conduct, candidates often reveal they've turned down an offer. To help the candidates understand why the job offer did not resonate with them, we discuss their reasons. The most common reasons why job offers are declined have remained consistent.

Hiring process lacked consistency

Consistency and communication are two critical elements of a successful hiring process. If a candidate detects inconsistencies during the interview process or experiences long delays or unclear communication, they often decline the offer. This can be resolved by utilizing a consistent hiring process, outlined in Chapter 1.

Job didn't show growth potential

The new opportunity didn't provide training, personal development, additional responsibilities, or a distinct avenue for growth. In this competitive job market, candidates want to increase their marketability by learning new things and want to have a plan for the next step in their career. It's important to stress the future career path, training provided, and personal development offered.

Family emergency

There are times when family emergencies take precedence over a career change. If this is a temporary situation, attempt to negotiate a delayed start date. If the company is not willing to offer alternatives and family is a priority for this candidate, they may determine the culture of the company is not a good match.

Team dynamics

When coworkers come across as aggressive, stubborn, or rude during the interview process, the candidate may have concerns because this is when they should be on their best behavior. This could predict future conflicts or a high-stress environment. Panel interviews can prevent an individual involved in the hiring process from sabotaging your ability to attract the best talent. Each person should understand their role and needs to be at their best when others are involved in the interview process.

Company culture

If the company culture is negative or if the company culture seems too modern or too traditional for a candidate's liking, they may not be happy working there every day. They will spend the major part of their day at work, and if they do not sense an overall positive environment, they will reject an offer. Company culture often ranks above compensation as the main reason candidates accept an offer. During the interview process, questions about the type of culture they prefer are pertinent to determine if this candidate is a fit or will end up being a costly turnover statistic.

Mission statement not accurate

Candidates are often drawn to a company's mission statement because it aligns with what's important to them. Too often they conduct additional research, read reviews, or talk to current employees and realize the mission statement is not a true reflection of the reality of working for this company. This is one more reason why candidates should have the opportunity to interact with their peers both before and after they receive an offer. The department they're working for could 100 percent reflect the mission statement, and having lunch with a coworker during their two-week notice period could confirm it.

Offer not lucrative

Money is not the only reason to accept a new job, but it does enter the decision-making process. If a candidate determines that the salary is much lower than market value and is not able to negotiate a higher salary, they will reject the offer. There is always an opportunity to revise the offer to be more competitive, which shows the candidate how much they are valued.

Offer too lucrative

You may be thinking why someone would turn down a job because the salary was too high. When money is well above average, it could be "combat pay" because the manager or working environment is that difficult. Candidates will often research the retention rate of past employees and decide to walk away. If there is a negative situation the newly hired candidate will face, discuss the situation during the interview process, so the candidate can make an informed decision up front and not learn of the issues by their own research.

Job doesn't align with core values

Candidates have core values that are part of their DNA. It's important that the values of a company don't clash with the values of the candidate. For example, it would be very difficult for an environmentalist to work for a coal company. That's an extreme example, but it's important that your interview process reveal the core values of prospective candidates so you both can decide if the core values of your company and this candidate align. You don't want to waste your valuable time or theirs.

No work-life balance

This is an area that is extremely important to Millennials who now represent over 50 percent of the workforce. They do not live to work like the Baby Boomers; they work to live. They feel a great job should give you space and time to breathe, to be yourself, and to be happy. If the new job expects them to put in every waking hour working, checking email, traveling, or meeting clients after hours, the candidate will rethink accepting this job. If your goal is to attract Millennials, it's important to rethink how you can embrace the concept of work-life balance.

Job seems too easy

If the job is too easy, chances are it is a lateral move and does not represent career advancement. The candidate will be concerned that the job will not be challenging enough and will not enhance their marketability. If this job is a stepping-stone to career advancement and that is explained to the candidate, they will consider accepting an offer.

Other offers are pending

In this competitive job market, candidates often receive multiple offers. They will weigh them against each other to accept the one that best aligns with their career goals. Never pressure a candidate to accept your offer, or you will eventually lose them. Make every attempt to show them how your opportunity aligns with not only what they want to do right now, but where they want the career to advance in the future.

Job seems too difficult

If a candidate accepts a job that is too difficult or complex, they begin to worry if they can accomplish the performance objectives of the position. If there is no time to learn and adapt to a higher level of responsibility, this is not a job they will accept.

Commute is too far

When a candidate considers the amount of time they will spend commuting to and from work, they realize the 10- to 12-hour days will take away from their personal life.

Some of the challenges that you face in getting your candidate to accept the offer you present may come from your competitors. Other companies may lure your candidate away with a higher-paying position or with additional benefits. How would you respond? You may also face a challenge in aligning the candidate's goals, requirements, and timing with the needs, requirements, and timing of the hiring authority. Perhaps the candidate's priorities have changed since they first spoke with you, and they have decided they want to stay in their current position a bit longer and hope to be promoted. What would you do? Or perhaps you have a candidate who is very interested in the role you're offering, but they would be working in a remote location which requires a long and inconvenient commute. How would you approach reconciling the needs of the candidate and the hiring authority?

In this chapter, I provide guidance on how to manage the most common challenges you may face when extending job offers to your candidates. Prepare yourself to manage these challenges, then implement the step-by-step process I've outlined for how to present a job offer that will be accepted. I also provide advice on how to ensure that your candidate resigns so that you can be better assured they have accepted your position.

Overcoming competitor challenges

Once a candidate begins the interview process with you, it is quite common for them to reach out to their network and learn of other job opportunities. As a result, it is not unusual for them to receive more than one job offer—and often a counteroffer from their current employer. This can happen before, during, or even after you extend a job offer. Often candidates will continue to interview during their two-week notice period, even after they've accepted your offer. If they receive another job offer and feel it is more aligned with what's important to them, your offer is declined.

Here are a few suggestions to help you stay informed and then prepare yourself for offers from competitors or a counteroffer from their current employer.

1. Know if your candidate is interviewing elsewhere

Be sure you know if your candidate is actively interviewing. Most candidates will schedule interviews for other positions but will not inform you unless you ask. If candidates seem reluctant to respond to your queries, explain how it benefits them to tell you what other jobs they are considering. You might say, "I don't want to duplicate any of your efforts to find a job. When I'm aware of your other interviews, it helps me fine-tune my efforts on your behalf." Knowing whether your candidates are interviewing elsewhere helps you prepare yourself and the hiring authority to either figure out a strategy for effectively selling against the other offers or eliminating this candidate from consideration.

2. Understand what competitors are offering

If you are working with a highly qualified candidate, it is likely that they will receive other job offers. As they may be reluctant to share this information with you, you should be candid and tell them that it is common for in-demand talent to receive multiple offers. Let them know that as their recruiter, you are skilled in negotiations and can help them compare offers so that they can better decide which opportunity is right for them. Knowing what they are being offered helps you and the hiring authority determine whether you can revise your offer to have the best chance of this candidate accepting your offer.

We once represented a candidate who received an offer $15,000 higher than our offer, but the bonuses were based on company profits and not guaranteed. In addition, they did not pay for family coverage, which would cost the candidate in excess of $15,000 per year. When our candidate compared the two offers, he realized our offer was the better decision, even if the salary was lower.

3. Prepare yourself for a counteroffer from their current employer

You don't want to advance a candidate who will accept a job offer you provide to them and then turn around and accept a counteroffer from their current employer. In fact, some candidates interview for another job in order to improve their ability to negotiate their next promotion and raise from their current employer. To make sure you don't find yourself in that situation, ask candidates if they would accept a counteroffer which would represent their next promotion and raise from their current employer. Some candidates will admit they would accept a counteroffer. If so, advise them that it's better for them to ask for their next promotion and raise now instead of negatively impacting the trust that exists between them and their current employer. Explain that they may negotiate a raise and promotion, but when future promotions are available and the employer knows this person was interviewing, the promotion may be offered to a peer who was not interviewing.

If your candidate is not successful in negotiating a promotion or raise from their current employer, they are much less likely to accept a counteroffer if one is extended after they've accepted your offer. They are now insulted that they had to threaten to leave in order to get the promotion and raise they deserved.

There are two questions you should ask during your interviews to prevent your candidate from accepting a counteroffer. When you ask your candidate if they will accept a counteroffer and they say, "I won't get one" or "I would never accept a counteroffer," that isn't enough information for you to sell against a counteroffer. Ask your candidate, "Why?" Then write their answer down verbatim and read it back to them. Explain that when they get a counteroffer, you are going to remind them of what they just said to you. Make sure the reasons they provide are not just about money and advancement because that describes a counteroffer. The other reasons they provide will not be solved by a promotion and raise.

Changing jobs is an emotional decision that takes most candidates out of their comfort zone, and the entire process is not easy. Their current employer knows them better than you do and also knows what buttons to push to make them feel guilty or indispensable. When your candidate obtains the counteroffer, which represents their next promotion and raise, they may become tempted to accept it. The best way to sell against a counteroffer is to read back what they said to you about why they would never accept a counteroffer. Their own words are much more powerful than anything you could say.

In addition, always ask candidates to list the five things they'd change about their current job if they were their boss. These reveal the real reason they are looking for another job because they will list things that are out of their control. When you also remind them of these five things, it solidifies their reasoning for accepting your offer and turning down the counteroffer.

4. Continue to clarify priorities with your candidate and quantify their answers

You are working with people on both sides of your recruiting process. As a result, life happens and the priorities and timing of your candidate often change. During every conversation continue to make sure nothing has changed. The simple question, "Has anything changed since the last time we talked?," is an easy way to start uncovering changes. Also quantify your candidate's level of interest on a scale of 1 to 10. If the answer is anything but 10, ask what would make their answer a 10. If your candidate's level of interest is low, it's better to pull them from the interviewing process before they receive a job offer.

Overcoming candidate challenges

When you interview a candidate for the first time, you are a stranger they don't know or trust. Often their answers are guarded because no rapport has been established. As you interact with a candidate, they begin to open up to you. They will share their priorities, goals, and any concerns they might have. Keep in mind that circumstances change, and so a candidate's priorities might change over time as well. When priorities change, the candidate's intention to change jobs may be put on a back burner, or the job you are offering may not align with their changed priorities. The job opportunity you're representing is no longer the career move they most desire.

You also need to consider the importance of their spouse and/or family in their decision. Spouses have a great impact on major decisions, and of course changing jobs is a major decision. Too often candidates do not discuss the details of a new opportunity until very late in the interviewing process. If the job involves longer hours, more travel, a longer commute, or could inconvenience the spouse in any way, the spouse may convince your candidate to decline the offer and wait for something better.

Here are a few suggestions to help prepare you for challenges that may occur based on the candidate's changing priorities, timing, or concerns from their family members.

1. Make sure you understand your candidate's priorities

Determining what is most important to your candidate is an ongoing process. If you've established rapport and trust with your candidate, they will be more inclined to share their goals and motivations—as well as questions and concerns—with you. Checking in with your candidate regularly shows them that you understand that circumstances and priorities change, and that they can be open and honest with you.

I remember representing a woman who was Vice President of Human Resources at a company but was interested in relocating to Chicago to be closer to her grandchildren. Halfway through the interviewing process, her mother was diagnosed with advanced cancer. She decided to put her relocation plans on hold so she could help care for her mother. When her mother passed away two years later, she ended up moving to Chicago. As a result of the relationship we had developed previously, she felt comfortable working with us and sought us out to help her find a new position in Chicago.

At the end of the day, recruiting is a relationship-building business, and when you take the time to build rapport and trust with your candidates, they will refer other top talent to you and utilize your services in the future.

2. Quantify your candidate's interest in the role

During every conversation with your candidate, make sure you are asking them if anything has changed since you last spoke. It also helps to ask them to quantify their level of interest on a scale of 1 to 10. In addition, ask them to rank your job against any other opportunities they may be considering. They may rate your job a 9, which makes you happy, until they rate another opportunity a 10.

3. Hit red flags head on

As recruiters, we want our candidates to accept offers we present. Therefore, we can sometimes dismiss or overlook red flags or information that a candidate provides that we don't want to hear. In the recruiting profession it's important *not* to have selective hearing. This is especially common when a candidate has successfully progressed through the interviewing process and becomes a frontrunner. However, red flags don't disappear as you get closer to a job offer. In fact, they end up front and center and will often result in a declined offer.

Early in my career, a candidate I was representing expressed their concern to me that everyone in the Accounting Department was much older than they were. Rather than address the concern the candidate had about working with older coworkers, I explained that the reason why the coworkers were older was that once hired, employees became engaged and retained and as a result were promoted to more senior positions. When this candidate received the job offer, she declined, sharing "I didn't feel comfortable working with people who were all twice my age. I socialize with my current coworkers and don't see that happening at this job." If I had asked more questions about why she was concerned about the older coworkers, this candidate would have been pulled from the interviewing process, and I would have saved the time and embarrassment of advocating on her behalf with the hiring authority.

Red flags and problem areas don't disappear; in fact they become more problematic as the interviewing process continues. Whenever a red flag surfaces, ask questions to ensure that you understand what the candidate said and how it will impact their decision-making process. While some red flags will be deal-breakers, others will not prevent a candidate from accepting a job or prevent a hiring authority from extending a job offer. It's your job as a recruiter to identify red flags, address them head on, and make your decisions based on the answers you receive from your candidate.

4. Ask if candidates regret leaving any past employer

When you interview a candidate with over 10 years of experience, ask them if they ever regretted leaving one of their past jobs and why. This provides you with great insight into the type of job they will accept without hesitation.

In this competitive job market, companies are hiring back great employees who left. If you're a third-party recruiter, contact this past employer, let them know you're representing one of their past employees, and inquire if they would consider hiring them back. Most companies can get back to you quickly to let you know if the candidate is eligible to be rehired.

5. Understand timing

As we discussed in Chapter 4, timing is everything in recruiting. If timing is not right for your candidate, they will decline any offer extended. Timing must be clarified from your first conversation and subsequently throughout the interviewing and hiring process. If your candidate's timing changes, you need to proactively address it. Ask additional questions to clarify your understanding of the new time frame, and then take appropriate actions with both your candidates and your hiring authorities.

6. Align the candidate's spouse

When a relocation is involved, clarify that the person's spouse, partner, or significant other is on board with the move. Even when the candidate is 100 percent in favor of the move, they will decline an offer if it threatens important relationships. Whenever possible, offer to answer any questions the spouse may have about the area, schools, or job market so you have a chance to determine their support early in the interview process.

Determine why they are interested in relocating, because the stronger the reason, the more apt they are to relocate. Have information sent to their home from the local chamber of commerce, school district (if they have children), Better Business Bureau, and any other brochures highlighting the location. Listen to their interests and put in the extra effort to identify private softball clubs, dance studios, or anything that personalizes the information for both your candidate and their family. If the company plans to fly out the spouse to visit the location, make sure you obtain a copy of the agenda, so the visit enhances and doesn't sabotage your candidate's high level of interest in relocating.

7. Clarify their commute parameters

Candidates often interview for jobs that are beyond where they prefer to commute, hoping or expecting that the hiring authority will accommodate them if they are the best candidate. Most candidates know how long they are willing to commute. They may interview outside of their comfort zone, but when they think about commuting to and from work every day, they often decide to decline an offer. Longer commutes are also more expensive when you consider wear and tear on a car, tolls, gas, and parking expenses. Even public transportation is more expensive for a longer commute. This always becomes part of the consideration when accepting a new job.

When the topic of commute is brought up in the conversation, ask your hiring managers if there is a chance to work virtually, if there are carpool opportunities, or if they can offset commuting costs or provide transportation.

Overcoming hiring authority challenges

A job opportunity that represents a candidate's next logical career move can be very enticing, but their excitement can diminish rapidly if they discover they have better bonuses, incentives, or benefits at their current employer. Many companies have very high deductibles, so if a candidate has great insurance with family coverage in their current role, they may decline an offer if the benefits at the new company are more expensive and don't offer family coverage. Candidates may also decline a job offer if their cost for benefits is deducted out of their net pay versus pre-tax dollars or if their current doctors are not covered under the new insurance. Candidates may also decline jobs that offer less paid time off than their current company.

If a candidate has a planned vacation, they would more than likely still qualify for their vacation pay from their current employer. The new employer would need to negotiate the vacation time off without pay as part of their offer.

Additionally, candidates may reject a job offer if they are being asked to relocate. If a job opportunity involves a relocation, the candidate faces two major life changes: changing their job and changing where they live. These are both extremely stressful decisions that may lead your candidate to ultimately decline your job offer. I have experienced this situation firsthand. I represented a candidate who wanted to move near her mother to help take care of her. She sold her house, enrolled her daughters in a new school, put the down payment on a condo, and was thrilled about her raise with better benefits. The day the moving vans showed up at her house, she sent them away. When I called her, she explained her cat had died and that it was bad karma and she couldn't move. In speaking with her, I assured her that I had worked with candidates in her situation many times before and that she just needed an extra week to tie up loose ends. I even called the employer, who agreed to push her start date back a week. However, at the end of the day, the two major life changes proved too much, and my candidate decided to decline the move and job offer.

Here are a few suggestions to help you discover and then prepare yourself for challenges that may come up based on challenges presented by a change in benefits or a job requiring relocation.

1. Become a benefits expert

The cost of health care continues to escalate and has become an important consideration when accepting a new job. You must understand your candidate's current coverage, deductibles, individual contribution, and type of plan to determine if your candidate can keep their current doctors and if the company offers individual or family coverage. Eligibility also impacts whether a candidate will accept a new job. If there is a waiting period, determine if the new company will offset the costs of COBRA or interim health benefits.

2. Define the reasons for a relocation

Many candidates want to move to a warmer climate because they're tired of winter. Other candidates want to relocate to a bigger city thinking there are more opportunities for career growth. These are both good reasons to relocate, but there must be more. A candidate may not like winter but may reconsider when they realize they are leaving their family, friends, and the changing seasons. Many candidates want to relocate to a bigger city but don't realize the increased cost of living, which often causes them to reconsider the move.

The primary reasons for relocation are a lower cost of living, a new job offering more money, preferred location, significant other, military service, marriage, children, or moving back home. There are many sites online that calculate the cost of living from one location to another. Share this information with your candidate early in the interviewing process. If your candidate has always dreamed of living in California, share the cost of living, taxes, and other relevant data. When a candidate is moving back home to be closer to family, very rarely does the relocation prevent them from accepting a job offer.

How to extend a job offer

There is always competition for top talent, which is why more attention should be given to the way an offer is extended. In this competitive market, I suggest that the candidate's new manager first extend the job offer in person in order to provide a warm welcome to the company. This should be followed by a written letter or email communicating the details of the offer.

When providing the verbal offer, the hiring manager should encourage questions and discuss the topic of counteroffer. It is important to remind the hiring manager that counteroffers from a candidate's employer can come late in the two-week notice period or even after your new hire has started. Making them aware of the competition they could face from their new hire's previous employer provides the motivation to onboard, nurture, and encourage their new employee.

Write a formal offer letter

While you are not legally required to provide an offer letter, many talent acquisitions professionals have adopted the practice of sending an offer letter to every hire. An offer letter helps to clarify key details and can help your company stand out if your candidate receives multiple job offers. The tone should be positive, making the candidate feel welcome, and should communicate excitement about adding them to your team. Explain clearly what actions your candidate needs to take, such as printing the letter, signing it, and sending it back to your office.

If written properly, an offer letter provides you with legal protection. It also ensures the candidate is informed and can successfully perform the responsibilities of the job they're accepting. There are eight primary sections of an offer letter, as shown in Figure 5.1.

Figure 5.1 Sample Offer Letter

9/28/20XX

Jodi Campbell
1234 Kingsway Avenue
Chicago, IL 60601

Dear Jodi,

It is my pleasure to extend the following offer of employment to you on behalf of TJJ & J Enterprise (the "Company"). This letter sets forth the basic terms and conditions of your employment.

Before the start of your employment with the Company, it's important to understand the terms of the employment. Please review the terms set forth in this letter carefully, and do not hesitate to make inquiries where necessary. If you have any questions, please contact Tyler Johns.

By signing this letter, you are agreeing to the following terms:

1. Your effective date of hire will be 10/12/20XX.
2. You will be paid an annual base salary of $110,000.00, less regular payroll deductions (payable as $4,538.00 semi-monthly), which covers all hours worked.
3. You will receive an override of 5% of the net sales of your team, paid quarterly.
4. Benefits are effective your first day of employment and are 100% paid by the company.
5. As an employee of the Company, you will become knowledgeable about confidential or proprietary information related to the operations, products and services of the Company. Similarly, you may have confidential or proprietary information from prior employers that should not be used or disclosed to anyone at the Company. You will be required to read, complete and sign the Company's standard employee confidentiality agreement and return it to the company on or before your start date. In addition, the

Company asks that you comply with any existing or continuing contractual obligations that you have with your former employers. By signing this offer letter, you represent that your employment with the Company will not breach any agreement you have with any third party.

6. Your job title will be Vice President of Sales and your duties will be to manage our current Sales Team, hire additional Account Executives, establish new territories and increase sales and profits. You will report directly to our Director of Operations, Jayden Ryne. You may be assigned to other duties as needed, and your duties may also change on reasonable notice, based on the needs of the Company and your skills.

7. By initialing this item, you agree to read and review the Company's employee handbook, which outlines your employee benefits and company policies and procedures. However, the Company reserves the right to change these policies and procedures.

8. This offer letter represents the entire agreement between you and the Company. This agreement supersedes any prior arrangement, representations, or promises of any kind whether oral, written, expressed or implied between you and the Company. This agreement constitutes the full agreement between you and the Company and cannot be changed unless in writing by the President of the Company.

9. If you agree with the above outline, please sign below. This offer is effective for five business days.

We look forward to having you join our team. To confirm your agreement with and acceptance of these terms, please sign one copy of this letter and return it to Jayden Ryne.

Sincerely,

_____

Carson Grochowski, VP of HR

I agree to the terms of employment set forth in this letter.

_____

Jodi Campbell

_____

Date

1 **Job title and description:** Include the exact job title, direct supervisor, primary functions of the job, and performance objectives.

2 **Start date and work hours:** This includes the agreed-upon start date. It also includes what days and hours the candidate will work. If the job is remote or there are no set hours, that information will be included in this section.

3 **Compensation:** This should include the salary amount, how and when wages are paid, the method of payment, and information on incentives or bonuses if applicable.

4 **Benefits and terms:** Benefits should include insurance information, vacation or PTO days, costs (pre- or post-tax), and eligibility. The benefit packet could be attached to the offer letter.

5 **Statement of at-will employment:** At-will employment allows the employee the right to quit at any time. It also allows the employer to fire a candidate at any time for any reason. However, the employer must show documentation outlining the employee's performance issues and efforts to improve the performance, or specific details on the issues that led to the termination. This documentation should be kept in the employee's personnel file and, if possible, should be signed by both the employer and employee. Employees also have an obligation to perform the functions of their job and not disclose confidential company information. It's also recommended that employees submit a two-week notice when they resign.

6 **A confidentiality agreement or noncompete clause:** This is signed by the candidate wherein they agree not to work for a direct competitor for a specific time frame after they leave the company.

7 **A list of any contingencies:** This section is for any conditions that must be met for the candidate to be officially hired, such as passing a drug or background check.

8 **Deadline for formally accepting the job:** The letter should include instructions and a deadline for the signed offer letter to be returned. Information in offer letters should be read and approved by legal counsel.

Helping your candidate resign

In this competitive, candidate-driven market, there are new realities regarding resignations. Changing jobs has a major impact on a candidate's life. While they may be excited about the opportunity their new position provides, they may also feel a sense of loyalty to their current employer. It may seem awkward, but you will want to confirm that your candidate has handed in their resignation. Often candidates do not hand in their resignation until they obtain more than one job offer. Provide your candidates with sample resignation

Figure 5.2 Sample Resignation Letter

9/28/20XX

CEO
ABC Company
710 N Main Street
Chicago, IL 60601

Dear Jack,

Please accept this letter as notice of my resignation from my position as Sales Manager. My last day of employment will be October 9, 20XX. I've accepted an offer for a VP of Sales position with a company that is experiencing tremendous growth. My offer represents career growth, less travel, increased compensation, and better benefits.

It has been a pleasure working for you over the last three years. One of the highlights of my career was landing three accounts which ended up becoming three of our top five revenue generating clients. I also hired, trained, and mentored two new Account Executives who are poised for a record year.

I wish you much success and would like to help with the transition of my responsibilities so my departure will not negatively impact sales or profits. I am available to recruit and train my replacement and will make certain all sales reports are finalized before my last day of employment.

Jack, thank you again for the opportunity to work for ABC Company. I wish you record sales next year and look forward to staying in touch. You can email me anytime at jodi@somedomain.com or call me at 555-555-5555.

Sincerely,

Jodi Campbell

letters that don't burn bridges but provide reasons that will help them gracefully separate from their previous employer. I have provided a sample resignation letter in Figure 5.2.

Once they confirm they have resigned, inform them that you can now check their references at their current place of employment. Confirming that a resignation has been given is one more strategy to ensure that not only will offers be accepted, but that your candidates have resigned and will show up on their start date. Always ask your candidate for referrals of other talent at their company. If they refer their coworkers to you, they will be much less likely to accept a counteroffer.

Summary

Obtaining a job offer for a recruited candidate should be your reward for a job well done, but unfortunately, a recruiter's work doesn't end there. This chapter taught you how to prepare yourself to face challenges that come up when extending an offer. You've learned to always ask if anything has changed since your last conversation and the importance of quantifying all answers provided. Lastly, you learned the value of an offer being put in writing and the benefits of helping your candidate write their resignation letter. When you follow the suggestions in this chapter, the offers you extend will be accepted!

Key takeaways

- Most candidates will schedule interviews for other positions but will not inform you unless you ask.
- Knowing whether your candidates are interviewing elsewhere helps you prepare yourself and the hiring authority.
- If you are working with a highly qualified candidate, it is likely that they will receive other job offers. Ask candidates if they would accept a counteroffer from their current employer.

- During every conversation ask your candidates, "Has anything changed since the last time we talked?," to uncover any possible changes.

- Quantify your candidate's interest level on a scale of 1 to 10.

- Identify red flags, address them head on, and make your decisions based on the answers you receive from your candidate.

- When a relocation is involved, clarify that the candidate's spouse, partner, or significant other agrees with the move.

- The commute always becomes part of the consideration when accepting a new job.

- There is always competition for top talent, which is why more attention should be given to the way an offer is extended.

- An offer letter helps to clarify key details and can help your company stand out if your candidate receives multiple job offers.

- Provide your candidates with sample resignation letters that don't burn bridges but provide reasons that will help them gracefully separate from their current employer.

Endnote

1   Robert Half, "Why Job Seekers Fail to Commit," nd, https://www.roberthalf.com/blog/evaluating-job-candidates/why-job-seekers-fail-to-commit (archived at https://perma.cc/TD6V-WNSP)

Employ techniques to eliminate surprises

6

Surprises that occur during the recruiting process are rarely in the recruiter's favor. Hiring authorities may change their mind about what they are looking for in the perfect candidate, which means that you may need to revise your recruiting targets and plans. There are times when candidates accept a job offer that you extended but then continue to interview for other positions. Often candidates receive another job offer from one of your competitors or are seriously considering a counteroffer they received from their current employer. You must then update the hiring authority to determine if they want to revise their offer or decide to let the candidate go and relaunch the search.

You can never assume that what a candidate is currently doing is what they want to do in the next job opportunity they accept. There are usually functions of their current job they do not enjoy, and they may want to eliminate those functions in their next job. In addition, most candidates will accept a job if it represents career advancement. If candidates are presented with job opportunities that are simply lateral moves, this often leaves candidates with the impression that the recruiter's key concern is to satisfy the needs of hiring authorities. When this happens, candidates will question your loyalty and will in return feel no loyalty to you as their recruiter. The most unfortunate surprise occurs when the candidate accepts a more suitable position as a result of their own search, and the recruiter is left without a candidate and a disappointed hiring authority.

Everyone in the recruiting process is human, and humans are prone to changing their minds; surprises are inevitable. With that said, recruiters can reduce the number of these frustrating surprises by developing trust and rapport with both hiring authorities and candidates. Establishing that level of rapport demands a high-tech *and* high-touch approach. Technology can screen in candidates who map to keywords, but don't make the mistake of thinking that a search result is a connection. This is where you must become involved and employ a high-touch approach with all prospective candidates. Take time to ask questions and listen to your candidates' answers in order to accurately determine their priorities. This is how you begin to develop rapport and trust. Better communication practices will result in fewer unwelcome surprises.

In this chapter, I outline a number of high-touch recruiting techniques to help you develop rapport and trust, which will eliminate most surprises when working with your candidates and hiring authorities. You will learn the proper techniques to pre-close as well as prepare and debrief not only your candidates but also your hiring managers. In addition, you will understand how checking references and quantifying interest levels helps you drastically reduce candidate "ghosting" and improves your ability to successfully fill more requisitions with the best talent.

Clarify mutual understanding by pre-closing

Communicating with clarity and transparency by "pre-closing" ensures that you and your candidate share a common understanding of what is being offered by the hiring authority. So often we are listening but not really hearing what candidates or hiring authorities have said. Pre-closing is a technique used to clarify and ensure mutual agreement on important words used in job requisitions or during conversations. For example, when asking a hiring authority about a specific requirement, clarify the definition and restate the answer to make sure you both agree and understand what was stated. When you share a common understanding of what was said and agreed upon during your conversations, you have taken an important step toward developing rapport and trust.

In Figure 6.1, clarifying what was meant by the word *dependable* is critical to finding the right candidate for the position. Without this clarification, you might have sought out candidates who could be relied upon to do the job well but were ultimately not the best fit. Another example could be realizing a candidate's commute would be extremely long and that they preferred a job where they could split their time between working in the office and working from home. This pertinent information may not have been discussed in your initial interview because the distance of their commute was not addressed. By using the pre-closing technique and clarifying the meaning of a critical qualification (someone who shows up for work every day), you can now better serve the needs of the hiring authority and potential candidates.

Repeating what your client says may also help cast a light on other potential areas of misunderstanding, leading your client to fine-tune other aspects of the job requisition. This will ultimately save you a lot of time in your efforts to find the right candidates and help prevent your hiring authorities from screening out candidates you know are qualified. As a result, you will schedule interviews for a much higher percentage of the candidates you represent.

When it comes to pre-closing your candidate, it is critical to clarify important words used in describing what they are looking for in a

Figure 6.1 Hiring authority pre-close

Hiring authority	It's important that I hire someone who is dependable.
You	I want to make sure I understand what you mean by dependable. Are you looking for someone who does whatever it takes to get a job done?
Hiring authority	No, I'm looking for someone who shows up for work every day. We have an attendance problem in our department.

Figure 6.2 Candidate pre-close

Candidate	I'm looking for a job where I can advance.
You	Are you asking me to get you a job that you can grow into versus out of?
Candidate	No, advancement to me is making more money. Job title doesn't matter to me.

new role, such as *advancement* or *compensation* (see Figure 6.2). By not clarifying the definition of words used, you risk misunderstanding your candidates' goals and may set up interviews that do not reflect what is most important to them. As a result, candidates don't show up for the interviews you arrange.

Pre-closing candidates by clarifying what important words mean prevents this from happening and dramatically reduces the likelihood of candidates failing to show up at an interview, or what is commonly referred to as a "no-show" or "ghosting."

Often when you are pre-closing your hiring authorities or candidates, throughout the interviewing process you realize things have changed. This could include timing, the performance objectives, credentials now desired, or the priorities of either your hiring authority or candidates. Changes or surprises can often sabotage your ability to successfully fill requisitions. As a general practice, I recommend regularly checking in with your hiring authorities and candidates by asking "Has anything changed since the last time we talked?" This gives the opportunity for them to reflect, and if something has changed, you can then use the pre-close technique to clarify your understanding of the changes. I've often wondered why hiring authorities and candidates don't keep us informed of changes, but over the years I realized they rarely update you, unless you ask.

Prepare your candidate for the interview

According to a recent survey by Indeed, 83 percent of companies reported that they had been ghosted by candidates. Half of those candidates who admitted to ghosting employers failed to show up for their interview. Among the reasons candidates provided for ghosting, or failing to show up for interviews, was a lack of communication with their recruiter.[1] Preparing your candidate for the interview is a great way of developing rapport and trust while also helping the candidate feel more confident and prepared for their interview. Your preparation will also provide your candidates with a competitive advantage over other less-prepared candidates. So often, it's not the most qualified candidate who gets hired, it's the candidate who aces the interview, which is why this process is so important.

Before your meeting with your candidate, you will need to prepare. Understanding your candidate, their background, what they define as career growth, and their priorities helps you to eliminate any positions that represent a lateral move. Next, ensure that you thoroughly understand the job requisition and performance objectives. You need to be able to explain to your candidate how success will be measured and what criteria will be used to evaluate them after their first 6 to 12 months. Lastly, find out as much as you can about the interview process. If you are a third-party recruiter, you must be knowledgeable and thoroughly understand the details of the hiring process for each client you represent.

Clarify how many interviews will be conducted, the type of interview (i.e., phone, panel, individual), and who will conduct interviews (obtain their names the titles). Ask if your candidate will be required to complete any assessments, forms, or tests as part of the interview process. Also clarify if the hiring authority will conduct background or credit checks or drug testing. When my office was located in downtown Chicago and we knew our candidate was going to be given a drug screen, during our prep process we advised them not to eat an authentic Chicago-style hot dog. These famous hot dogs are traditionally served on a poppy seed bun. We discovered after having a few candidates fail their drug tests that poppy seeds come from the seedpod of the opium poppy. When harvested, the seeds can absorb opium extract, which is used to make opioid drugs. Poppy seeds go through a thorough cleaning before being processed for consumer use for baking, but they still may contain trace amounts of opiate residue. The concentration isn't enough to give any effects of opioids but can be enough to produce a false positive drug test. This information is just one example of the benefits of preparing the candidate.

If you tell a candidate you want to prep them, not all candidates will understand the benefit to them, and they may not be excited about the time and energy required. To increase their interest, don't use the word *prep*. Inform your candidates that you have information you'd like to share with them about the job, company, and interviewer that will provide them with a competitive edge. It's wise to tell them that there are other candidates who are being interviewed for this same position. Everyone wants what everyone else wants, which is why it's important for your candidates to know there is competition. Also, let them know that this is a perfect time to ask questions or voice any concerns they may have about the job or company. Encourage them to set up Google alerts on the company and conduct research before meeting. Suggest that they also write down the questions they plan to ask. If your candidate is currently working, schedule the interview prep at a time when they can talk openly. An effective interview prep should be a two-way conversation, which can only happen if they have a private office or if the prep is conducted after working hours. This is one process you never want to short-change because it prepares your candidates to be at their best during their interview, outshining other candidates. It also greatly reduces no-shows or ghosting, because your candidate feels informed, confident, and prepared.

Share details of the job and interview process: The first 15 minutes

The candidate interview preparation is broken down into two parts; each should last only about 15 minutes. The first 15 minutes should be spent first clarifying interview time, location, security measures, identification needed, additional paperwork to be filled out, testing or assessment completed, and so on. After covering interview logistics, you then outline the job responsibilities and review your candidate's qualifications. For example, when I am reviewing a job requisition with a candidate, I ask the candidate to share their level of experience for each job responsibility. I ask, "Have you done this before? What experience do you have that qualifies you for this responsibility?" and "Would you enjoy this as a function in your next job?" These questions reveal if you've made an appropriate match for your hiring authority and candidate.

Once the responsibilities are reviewed, I then ask the candidate to share any concerns or questions. It's better to uncover concerns or red flags prior to an interview. Next ask the candidate about their level of interest in the position on a scale of 1 to 10. If they respond with anything other than a 10, ask, "What would make it a 10?" As I'm completing the first part of the prep, I ask the most important question: "If you were to obtain an offer in the salary range we discussed, is this a job you would accept *today*?"

The most important word in that question is the word *today*. As we've discussed in prior chapters, timing has a great impact on your ability to successfully fill open requisitions. This is often where a candidate reveals that they have other interviews or offers pending. Ask your candidate to rank your job compared to others to determine whether you should proceed with this candidate or eliminate them from consideration.

Acceptable responses could include that the candidate wants to meet their direct boss, discuss their decision with their significant other, or experience the company firsthand. However, it's important that your candidate has a level of interest on a scale of 1 to 10 of at least a 7 for you to be confident they have a strong level of interest in the job.

If there is a strong reason that they would not accept an offer, it's in the best interest of both the candidate and hiring authority to cancel the interview. If you don't, chances are the candidate may fail to show up for the interview because it is not a job they will accept.

Conducting a mock interview: The second 15 minutes

During the second 15 minutes of the candidate prep, teach your candidate how to respond effectively to interview questions. You are not providing them with answers, but you want to make sure they are comfortable with the process of interviewing. In my experience, most people are not comfortable interviewing for a job unless they have sales experience or have had many job changes in their past. Most people tend to be reserved in answering interview questions for fear they will be perceived as overly confident. Unfortunately, this reticence is often mistaken for a lack of enthusiasm about the position and may lead the hiring authority to eliminate them from consideration.

To help your candidate feel more at ease when sharing their achievements and experience, I suggest they view the interview as an audition, where they are auditioning for the job rather than fact-finding. I often compare the interview to the process an actor goes through when vying for a role in a movie. The actor must perform during a screen test, so the director envisions them as the perfect actor for a role in their movie. The interview is the screen test, and the candidate's goal is to convince the hiring authority that they are the perfect fit for the job. They want to leave a lasting impression, so the hiring authority envisions them in the job and begins to compare other candidates to them.

Next role-play with your candidate to make them more comfortable with the interviewing process. Be careful not to correct candidates or provide them with answers to interview questions. This could also negatively impact the rapport and trust you have been establishing with them. Ask them questions and listen to their answers as if you were the hiring authority. If an answer is negative or could cause your candidate to be screened out, switch roles with them and have them ask you the same question. When you repeat their answer, they will hear the negativity or issue and will understand why their answer should be revised. If you disagree with a candidate and tell them what to say, they may feel you are asking them to misrepresent the truth. Any revisions that are suggested must come from your candidate.

Also encourage candidates to prepare questions in advance that they will ask the interviewer. Teach them to ask questions that reveal the priorities of every person involved in the interviewing process. Priorities from one interviewer to the next can be very different depending on how much interaction they will have with this candidate if they are hired. An example of this type of question is "What is most important to you in the person you hire?" If candidates do not prepare questions in advance, they will often ask self-serving questions like "How much vacation do you offer?" One of the best questions a candidate can ask is "I'm interested in this position and confident I can do the job, but what's most important is what you think. Do you feel I have the experience and credentials necessary to do the job?" This allows your candidate to start out by restating their high level of interest and confidence in their ability to do the job before you find out if this interviewer has any concerns that could screen you out.

Interviewers will almost always start out by sharing positive feedback about the interview; however, if they use the word *but*, their concerns will follow. Prepare your candidates so they respond with "I can totally understand why you feel that way. Let me explain why that won't be a problem." If they effectively address the interviewers' concerns, they will often be forwarded to the next round in the interview process. If your candidate is ultimately screened out, the answer to this question provides them with the reason why they were screened out. This feedback will help your candidate improve their interviewing skills.

Prepare your hiring authority to interview

Much like candidates, not all hiring authorities will be excited about the idea of your wanting to prepare them for interviews. You would never use the words *interview prep* but would instead focus on how the discussion will help them attract the top talent they need to hire. Inform them that you know the five things the candidate would change about their current job if they were the boss, you know why they've made changes in the past, and you're aware of what is most important for them to make a job change today. Also share with the hiring authority why the candidate left previous positions. If the hiring authority is aware that the market is competitive, which most of them are, then they will welcome any information that will help them successfully interview and hire the best talent. Once they understand how the preparation will benefit them, they are much more likely to set time aside to talk with you.

Most hiring authorities are aware that they may need to compete for the most qualified candidates. However, it's important that you still explain the realities of the candidate-driven market and emphasize the need to sell the company and the job opportunity during their interview. Encourage your clients to discuss the company culture, core values, and tenure of current employees, as well as career advancement and training offered. These are the most important areas to the majority of today's workforce.

Avoid unwanted surprises by conducting candidate debriefs

Debriefing candidates after an interview with hiring authorities is the best way of assessing whether a candidate is truly interested in the role and if they are likely to be receptive to a job offer, should one be extended. A debriefing conversation will also help you improve your preparation for future candidates who interview with the same hiring authority.

Historically, candidate debriefs have been conducted before the client debrief, but this has changed in the candidate-driven market. If you've determined your hiring authority has a higher level of interest in the candidate than the candidate has in the opportunity, you should debrief the client first. This will help you overcome any problematic issues that may have occurred during the interview and can also provide you with additional selling points you can then share with your candidate during their debrief. If you're not sure who has the highest level of interest, debrief the candidate first.

To ensure that you are capturing information accurately, debriefs should be conducted immediately following a phone or face-to-face interview. One of the objectives of a debrief is to uncover any disparity between the information you provided to the candidate and the information provided by the hiring authority. Ask the candidate directly if the description of the position outlined by the employer matched the description that you provided to them. While these descriptions should be the same, asking this question helps you discover those instances when job specifications have changed and you were not informed.

Asking candidates questions about their interviews provides you with insight into the interviewing and hiring process. For example, you may have provided your candidate with a preliminary list of who would be interviewing them, but the interview went so well that additional individuals were included. Knowing who those additional people are and what positions/functions they represent provides you with a better understanding of how the role interacts with other functions or departments.

Candidate debriefs also help you quantify the candidate's level of interest in the position. Ask them if they think they would enjoy the job as described, and ask for their feedback about the interviewer. Also ask them to share any concerns about the job, company, or culture so you can discuss them with your hiring manager. Then ask your candidate if they provided any responses they wish they could take back based on the reaction of the interviewer. If you bring this up first with the client and explain that your candidate was concerned about their response, this often prevents their answer from becoming an issue. These answers together will help you quantify their interest in the position and help you provide feedback to your hiring authority. You should always ask your candidate to quantify their interest in the position on a scale of 1 to 10 to help you determine if your candidate will accept an offer. A candidate debrief form is provided in Figure 6.3.

Figure 6.3 Candidate interview debrief form

Candidate:	Candidate phone number:
Company:	Job order number:
Date of interview:	Position:

I'd like to ask you a few questions regarding the interview:

1. Whom did you talk to (phone interview) or meet with?

Name:	Title:	Time spent:
Name:	Title:	Time spent:

2. Was the position outlined by the employer the way I described it to you? Please share your understanding of the position and its responsibilities.

3. Can you perform the responsibilities of the job?

Give me three reasons why... (I ask you these questions because I want to reinforce your qualifications to the company when I follow up with them regarding your interview.)

A	
B	
C	

4. Would you enjoy the job?

5. Whom will you report to?

6. Can you work with that person?

7. Did the company impress you? Why or why not?

8. How long was your drive/commute?

9. Was compensation discussed?

YES	NO
What was discussed?	Close to the NO on $:
If money was discussed, was it acceptable to you?	Amount close to NO:
If not, why?	Other financial requirements:
What would be acceptable (close to NO on money)?	

10. **Were the benefits explained? Do you have any questions about them?**

11. **Did they discuss:**

YES   NO

Reviews

Raises

Promotions

Your career path

Any questions

12. **Do you have any reservations at all? If so, please explain.**

13. **Based on your information to date, do you want the job?**

14. **How did the employer leave it with you?**

15. **Did the employer request reference information? What reference names did you share?**

16. **You understand that I will do my best as an experienced negotiator to get you as much as possible. However, I don't want to price you out of the marketplace. Your minimum salary is confidential between you and me. As we discussed earlier, your minimum salary or pay rate requirement would be $X?**

17. **If the employer calls me with an offer of employment, I want your authorization to accept on your behalf and here's why:**
    - Companies like people who can make decisions.
    - It shows your confidence that you can do the job.
    - It shows your sincere interest in working for them.
    - The last thing I want to tell the company is that you want to think about it, because that raises doubts in their minds and they will continue to interview other people. Do I have your authority to accept?

18. **Do you understand that when you go to resign from your present employer, they may meet or exceed the terms of (company's name) offer of employment? What would you do?** (Stop talking and listen.)

19. **Send a follow-up letter or thank you card to the employer.**

    ● Thank them for the opportunity to interview.

    ● Express your confidence in doing the job.

    ● Give reasons why you can do the job.

    ● Express an interest in pursuing the opportunity and look forward to hearing from them soon.

20. **By the way, are there any other opportunities you are investigating at this time? How do they compare?**

21. **Rate this position on a scale from 1 to 10. If not 10, what would make it a 10?**

To prevent surprises, find out if your candidate has any other interviews or potential offers pending during the debrief process. If so, find out how your opportunity compares to others they are considering. Ask your candidate to rank the jobs they are considering from the one that most interests them to the least. Once you understand your candidate's level of interest, you can make an informed decision whether to advance them to the next round of interviews or remove them from consideration.

Avoid disappointed candidates by conducting hiring authority debriefs

After debriefing your candidate, it is important to check in with the hiring authority to quantify their level of interest in your candidate (see Figure 6.4). Again, if the hiring authority has a higher level of interest in hard-to-find top talent, you would debrief the hiring authority first. The hiring authority debrief helps you identify where your candidate ranks and uncovers any reservations the hiring authority may have about your candidate. If your candidate is interested in the position, you will start the debrief by making the case for why

Figure 6.4 Hiring authority interview debrief form

Company:	Hiring manager phone number:
Contact:	Title:
Candidate:	Position:

1. **Express candidate's interest and enthusiasm for position.**

   In discussing the interview with (candidate's name), I asked a series of questions, the first being "Are you interested in the job?" Candidate said, "I'm interested in the job because…"

Reasons why candidate wants the position:	
Reasons why candidate can do the job:	

2. **What did you like about (candidate's name)?**

   In your opinion at this point, do you feel that this person can do the job? YES/NO Why/why not:

   Do you have any reservations at all concerning (candidate's name)?

   Level of interest on a scale of 1 to 10 (10 being the highest):

3. **Address reservations, offer rebuttals, emphasize candidate's strengths:**

4. **Volunteer reference information:**

5. **Mr./Ms. (hiring manager name), are you prepared to make an offer at this time? If yes, complete offer information. If no, why? Get time frame for hiring decision.**

6. **Are you considering other candidates at this time?**

   How many:

   How does this person rank:

Pertinent offer information – contract		
Bill rate:	Paid when:	
Pay rate:	Paid when:	
Start date:	Start time:	Report to:
Location:	Proper attire:	
Additional instructions:		

Pertinent offer information – direct		
Salary amount:	Paid when:	
Commission/bonuses:	Paid when:	Based on:
First salary review:	Average increase amount / percentage:	
Start date:	Start time:	Report to:
Location:	Proper attire:	

Benefits		
MM:	HMO / PPO:	Dental:
Vision:	Life:	401K:
LTD:	STD:	EAP:
Profit sharing:	Tuition reimbursement:	Company car:
Sick days:	Expense account / details:	Other:

Additional benefit information	
Signing bonus amount:	
Benefits totally company paid:	If no, what monthly cost to employee?
Vacation first year:	Vacation after first year:
Benefit eligibility – Immediate | 30 days | 60 days | 90 days:	
Other:	

your candidate is a good fit for the position. You will talk about the confidence they have in their ability to do the job and their high level of interest in the overall opportunity. You then ask your hiring authority what they like about your candidate, if they feel your candidate can do the job, and finally you ask them to quantify their level of interest on a scale of 1 to 10. If they say anything but a 10, ask what it would take to make it a 10 and overcome any objections or concerns. You also want to find out where the hiring authority is in the interview process and confirm their target date to hire a new employee.

Inquire if there are other candidates being considered, and ask where your candidate ranks. The answers to these questions will help you provide feedback to your candidates, fine-tune your search, and can improve preparing future candidates. If your candidate is screened out, too often you are just told, "Your candidate was not a fit." That does not help you improve your recruiting process. A better question to ask your hiring authority would be "What was this candidate missing? I don't want to waste your time, and your answer will help me fine-tune my recruiting efforts."

I once had a hiring authority admit that my candidate was a perfect fit, but he didn't want to hire the first candidate he interviewed. He then asked me to set up additional interviews. I explained that I had sent in my best candidate first, because I knew this was a priority hire and the vacancy was causing other employees to take on additional work. I also informed my client that this candidate was actively interviewing, and there was no guarantee she would be available if he continued to interview. I asked for three interview times and a new extended target date to hire. The next day, the hiring authority called me with an offer and went to the top of their salary range to entice the candidate to accept. She did accept the job, and 10 years later was with the same company but had been promoted several times. Had I not provided the information during my debrief process, my hiring authority would have missed out on a peak performer who became an excellent engaged and retained asset to her company.

Check references to reveal discrepancies and present the best candidates

Reference checks will either hurt or help your candidates. Checking a candidate's references helps eliminate unexpected surprises by revealing inconsistencies, embellished skills, or other discrepancies that would disqualify them from consideration. Reference checks are the only way to determine if, in fact, your candidate has the level of skills, experience, and expertise shared in their interview.

At the same time, checking references helps you present candidates who will be the best fit for your hiring authorities. Speaking with a candidate's references allows you to verify information that was shared during your interview, as well as find out more about their on-the-job performance. I recommend calling at least one reference before presenting a candidate for consideration. Quoting information from a reference check allows you to schedule more interviews because you can provide your hiring manager with information from someone who has firsthand knowledge of your candidate's performance. In addition, it can also help overcome any concerns regarding your candidate.

Conducting a thorough reference check

When checking a reference, be sure to verify the title of the person who will provide the reference. When a candidate is concerned about their references, they might provide the name of a coworker or friend who misrepresents themselves as a supervisor. You can verify their title on LinkedIn or the company website, or ask to be transferred to the Human Resource Department. Whatever resources you utilize to confirm their title, ensure that you are speaking to a former supervisor or someone who can provide information about the candidate's performance.

Consistency is critical when checking references, so make sure that you are asking each reference the same questions. This will make it easier for you to compare competing candidates. The reference check information should follow a precise list of open-ended questions with follow-up clarification questions such as "Can you provide an example?" "How did they compare to others?" "Can you tell me more about their individual contribution to the project?" Also ask about areas needing improvement, problem-solving skills, attitude, teamwork, and their ability to get the job done. Whenever possible ask for examples of these traits, which also proves this person had firsthand knowledge of your candidate.

Obtain reference checks when it's most convenient for the contact, so they are not rushed and can speak openly. Start out by asking for general information like dates of employment, title, their relationships to the candidate, and basic responsibilities. Clarify the definition of words used so you don't misinterpret information. To prevent the conversation from getting off track, ask references to use a 10-point scale to determine the candidate's level of expertise in specific areas. Be diligent when entering facts, and make sure to enter your reference check form into your applicant tracking system or customer relationship management system. A reference check form is provided in Figure 6.5.

Figure 6.5 Reference check form

Consultant checking reference:

Name of candidate:	Date:
Company name:	Address:
Name of supervisor:	Title of supervisor:
Supervisor's phone number:	Candidate dates of employment:
Positions title(s) candidate held with company:	
Responsibilities (give examples of a typical day):	

Work Performance (as compared with others)
Were there any areas where the candidates excelled? Any particular strengths? Be specific:
Are there any areas that the candidate could use improvement? Any particular weaknesses? Be specific:
What was the candidate's greatest accomplishment? What impact did it have on the company?

Rate the following on a scale of 1 to 10 (10 being the highest rating):	
Technical skills:	Interpersonal skills:
Accuracy:	Efficiency:
Works well independently:	Works well with a team:
Attendance:	Punctuality:

Did this candidate work well with coworkers:	Did this candidate work well with management:
Reason left company:	Eligible for rehire YES/NO Why/why not:

Is there anything I haven't asked you that you would like to share?

Third-party recruiters

Ask the following question, after checking a reference:

"I take great pride in representing the best talent and verifying their credentials. I also represent some of the best companies and would love to become a backup to your current resources. What steps would I need to take to become a backup to your current resources for top talent?"

If not the correct contact: "Whom should I speak to regarding hiring? Will you transfer my call?"

There is another hidden benefit you will enjoy by checking references. The person you contacted to check references is in a position of authority and should become part of your lifetime professional network. They are usually well networked and could continue to be a valuable lifetime resource. A simple initial step is to connect on LinkedIn.

Overcoming challenges to reference checking

Some companies make it their policy to limit the information they provide on past employees to dates of employment and salary. This makes it very difficult to gain any insight into your candidate's on-the-job performance. While I respect these policies and the desire to protect employee records, I find it is helpful to sometimes ask a broader question that doesn't require any specific information as a response. For example, I might say, "I appreciate your policy, but my professional reputation is based on the quality of candidates I represent. Can I please ask you one question, off the record? If you were me, would you represent this candidate?" or "Is this candidate eligible for rehire?"

You may also face the situation where a past employer provides a negative reference because they are unhappy the candidate quit their company. Your candidates should let you know if a similar situation exists at any past employers. Sometime a disgruntled employer often admits that the candidate's performance was outstanding, which is why they were so upset when the candidate quit. When you are unable to obtain a positive reference from a candidate's direct report, ask the candidate for names of other managers who were aware of the quality of their work, and check those references.

Summary

With people on both sides of the recruiting process, surprises are inevitable, but you have learned that there are things you can do to eliminate surprises. Those processes include pre-closing, preparing, and debriefing both the candidate and client. To make this process easier to learn, take advantage of the forms provided.

Key takeaways

- Sometimes hiring authorities change job specifications, which means you must revise your recruiting efforts.

- Never assume what a candidate is doing now is what they want to do in their next job.

- Surprises can be reduced by developing rapport and trust with your candidates.

- Communicating with clarity and transparency by pre-closing will help you stay on the same page with your candidate and hiring authority.

- Repeating what your client says may also help reveal other potential areas of misunderstanding.

- When pre-closing candidates, clarify the definitions of words used.

- Consistently ask candidates and hiring authorities, "Has anything changed since the last time we talked?"

- Debrief the person who is most interested first (candidate or hiring authority).

- Conduct a thorough candidate debrief to determine level of interest and any concerns.

- Conduct a thorough client debrief to determine level of interest and any concerns.

- Reference checks can either help or hurt your candidate's chance of being hired.

- It's important to overcome challenges when checking references.

- When you can't obtain a positive reference from a candidate's direct report, ask the candidate for names of other managers who were aware of the quality of their work and check those references.

Endnote

1 Liz Lewis, "The Ghosting Guide: An Inside Look at Why Job Seekers Disappear," indeed blog, August 26, 2019, http://blog.indeed.com/2019/08/26/ghosting-guide/ (archived at https://perma.cc/5R4U-PXVQ)

Nurture candidates pre- and post-hire and obtain referrals

7

Too often recruiters are viewed simply as individuals who help companies hire the best talent while simultaneously helping candidates advance their careers. While these are two rewarding and important aspects of the recruiting profession, your career involves so much more. The level of success you achieve depends to a great extent on your ability to place candidates who become engaged, retained, and successful employees. Your job doesn't end when your candidate accepts a job offer. It is then that nurturing begins, so you can align your new hire before their start date and well beyond.

This chapter will describe nurturing behavior, why it's important even before your candidate's start date, and how to effectively nurture the candidates you place implementing a high-tech, high-touch approach. You will also learn how you benefit from nurturing, the value of mentorship, how to increase referrals, and how to build a strong employee referral program.

What is nurturing and why is it important?

There are many definitions of the word *nurturing*, but all agree that nurturing is a human trait and an integral part of our identity. Another common definition of nurturing is to support and encourage, or to train and educate. An example to further explain this concept would be children whose mothers were nurturing during their preschool years, as opposed to later in childhood. They experience increased brain structures associated with learning, memory, and stress response compared to children with less supportive mothers.[1] You can most definitely improve your candidates' chances to succeed by supporting them with nurturing.

You will help your candidates adapt to their new role by nurturing them, helping them feel comfortable, essential, and appreciated in their new workplace. Nurturing also plays a significant role when it comes to new employees' views on the leadership and vision of their new employer. As they understand the significance of the company's vision, it allows them to develop working strategies which align with that vision. Nurturing can build self-confidence, knowledge, and the drive to succeed.

With all the responsibilities involved in recruiting, asking recruiters to add employee nurturing to their roles may seem like asking too much. However, in addition to ensuring employee engagement and therefore your own success, you are in the best position to help support your candidate in those first few weeks. This is because your candidate already trusts you. As their recruiter, you were the person who originally established trust and rapport with them. When they begin their new job, you know more about your candidate than their new peers or supervisor does. Also, if they're experiencing any type of challenge, they likely will feel most comfortable talking to you. You are the person who sought them out and explained how this role would help advance their career. By helping smooth their transition to their new role, you deepen your relationship with your candidate and solidify your commitment to a solid overall candidate experience.

Align new hires before they begin

As discussed in previous chapters, the best candidates are likely to receive multiple job offers and counteroffers, and these offers may continue even after they have accepted a new role. More of the candidates who accept job offers will start if you nurture them in the two-week notice period (or longer) that proceeds their official start date. Implement the strategies to prevent counteroffers which were shared in prior chapters of this book, but also offer to help them with their letter of resignation by providing them with sample templates. Once your candidate has told you they've resigned, remember to thank them for letting you know because your hiring authority wanted a current reference but didn't want to call their current employer until they had handed in their notice. You will be shocked how often your candidate then admits they haven't handed in notice to their boss. Asking to check a current reference is the only way you can verify that your candidate has, in fact, handed in their notice.

As a recruiter, you are focused on filling open requisitions with top talent daily so it's easy to think of changing jobs as an easy process. However, think for a moment about the last time you were in the job market conducting your own search. You then remember how emotional it can be to change jobs. A job search is filled with highs and lows and can take even an experienced recruiter or talent acquisition professional out of their comfort zone. After you considered various opportunities, you finally accepted a job offer. But then you handed in your two-week notice and probably spent those next two weeks asking yourself a lot of questions. Did I accept a job too soon? Will I enjoy the work I'm assigned? Will I get along with my new boss? Will I fit into the company culture? Why haven't I heard anything since I accepted my offer? Should I accept the lucrative counteroffer I've been extended? I wonder if this job change is a mistake? After your candidates accept a job offer, they are also having second thoughts during their two-week notice. In addition, they may have family or friends telling them they could have negotiated a better compensation package, they may interact with a past disgruntled employee, or they may just begin to experience the fear of change.

In order to keep them engaged with you, remain in contact with them to address any apprehensions they may be experiencing. Create and implement a structured touch program between the day an offer is accepted and their first day of employment. Enter your action items in your applicant tracking system (ATS) or client relationship management system (CRM) to remind you of the follow-up actions you will take with your placed candidates. Keeping them engaged and connected with you is a great way to address any concerns. You want to make sure they are excited, informed, and looking forward to their first day of employment. Your candidates will be prepared, knowing exactly what to expect, and feel assured that the company, their new boss, and coworkers/peers are excited to welcome them to the team.

Another way to align candidates with the company before they formally begin is by encouraging the hiring manager, or one of your new hire's peers, to meet with them for lunch or dinner during their notice. This allows the new hire to develop rapport with their manager or peers and gives them an opportunity to ask questions. This also helps alleviate the possible fear of change and begins to help this candidate align with their new team and employer. If schedules don't allow for this type of meeting, ask the HR business partner or your hiring authority to set up a meeting with your candidate to welcome them to the company. During this meeting your candidate could be asked to complete their benefit or tax paperwork in advance of their start date. This provides another opportunity for your candidate to visit and become comfortable with their new place of employment. In addition to talking with your candidate throughout their notice period, also call them the night before their start date to wish them good luck.

Nurture placed candidates with a high-tech, high-touch approach

We repeatedly have stressed the importance of a high-tech, high-touch approach to help improve the overall candidate experience. There is no better time to accomplish this than when you are nurturing your candidate. Remember, there are three questions your candidates want answered: Can they trust you? Do you care about them? Do you deliver what you promise? When you continue to personally nurture your candidates after they accept a job offer, the answer to all three questions is yes. There are recruiters who place candidates and basically forget about them. In this candidate-driven market, it is more important than ever for you to make the time to nurture every candidate you place. Developing a long-term relationship with the candidates you place is also personally rewarding. It's gratifying to watch them advance in their careers and will often help motivate you to excel further in the recruiting profession.

Once your candidate begins their employment, it's important that you understand the details of the onboarding process, so you can answer any questions or direct them to the right sources of information. Your goal is to have your new hire prepared to contribute to their team as soon as possible. If there are other new hires also participating in the onboarding process, make sure they are introduced and interact with each other. Your company or client has one chance to make a great first impression on their new hire, which is why a high-tech, high-touch approach is so valuable. Make sure they receive a warm welcome upon arriving. They should be provided with technology affiliated with their job, as well as their username, password, and email address. Schedule follow-up contacts on your calendar to prove by your actions that you care about the success of the candidate you placed.

If you are a third-party recruiter who places temporary workers or contractors, you may be expected to handle the onboarding process. This is something you need to clarify up front with each client company. If you have provided a significant number of temporary workers or contractors to a company, consider the benefits of having someone from your staffing or recruiting firm on-site to handle onboarding, employee relations, time sheets, payroll, and any additional issues. This person would also be responsible for nurturing your employees. Making sure their first day is a positive and memorable experience will improve engagement, retention, and referrals of other candidates. Describe the work they will be doing so they understand the value of their role in helping the company achieve goals.

Another way a recruiter can help nurture their candidates is to develop a structured program to informally communicate with new hires. You want to keep the channels of communication open so you can help your candidate solve any small issues before they become big problems. Due to the demand for talent, candidates may continue to receive multiple offers or counteroffers or continue to interview even after they have accepted a position. Some counteroffers are extended when your candidate hands in their two-week notice, but often counteroffers are extended two, three, or even six months after your candidate is hired. Often the company was not able to replace your candidate, or the replacement they hired didn't work out. As a result, they pursue your candidate with a lucrative counteroffer. Continue to keep the lines of communication open so you can sell against accepting a counteroffer well after your candidate has started their new job. It's a good idea to ask them if they have heard from their past employer. If they say yes and share that they are having lunch together, warn them they are meeting to extend a counteroffer. Remind your candidate of the five things they wanted to change if they were their boss during your interview with them. This will help prevent them from accepting a counteroffer after your company has gone through the expense of onboarding and training and is now realizing a return on investment on your candidates.

How you benefit from nurturing

Your candidates' performance in the initial stages of their employment is a direct reflection on your ability as a recruiter to present and place candidates who are the best fit. While it certainly would be easier to simply focus on recruiting new candidates and leave the tasks of onboarding to the hiring authority, recruiters who help their candidates adjust to their new workplace see higher levels of engagement and retention of the candidates they place.[2]

Regularly connecting with your candidates also gives you an opportunity to ensure they understand the impact of their work. When employees feel their work is making a positive impact and they are developing their talents and skills, they will not end up as a costly turnover statistic.

Taking the time to nurture your candidates obviously benefits the candidates you place but will also benefit you by strengthening your reputation and relationship with hiring authorities. Nurturing candidates helps prevent turnover, which costs companies a fortune and has become one of the top priorities of companies worldwide. Further, you become a trusted partner who shares pertinent information about candidates that encourages them to mediate and prevent small problems from turning into larger ones. Hiring authorities learn they can trust you and know you will do whatever it takes to help the candidate you place succeed.

The value of mentorship

Modern mentorship programs are designed to support both the mentor and the mentee as they learn and grow on a professional and personal basis and are extremely valuable in that they extend beyond the initial onboarding process. A strong mentor-mentee relationship will help new hires learn from an experienced employee, while exposing the more seasoned employee to solutions and approaches to company objectives from the fresh perspective of a new employee. Mentoring also demonstrates to the new hire the benefits of an open culture where employees share knowledge, generate ideas, and work together to build a successful company.

Some of the additional benefits of being a mentee include practical advice, encouragement, and support. You learn from the experience of others. You also become more empowered to make decisions, confirm goals, and gain valuable insight into the next stage of your career. Some of the additional benefits of being a mentor include the development of leadership and management qualities, reinforcing your expertise, and increasing recognition and value to your employer. Mentors also benefit from a sense of fulfillment and personal growth.

Helping your candidate find a mentor in their new role shows your candidates that you don't place or hire them and then forget them. You are invested in ensuring they are happy and successful, and you can be trusted to be there for them. Your candidates will often not remember what you say to them, but they will always remember how you make them feel. Developing this relationship with them will ensure they refer friends or other coworkers to you.

Dramatically increase referrals

Your nurturing and follow-up process will lead to referrals of additional top talent. If a candidate has had a great experience working with you, they are likely to refer top talent to you. Technology has increased your candidate's professional and personal networks. There's a good chance that your new employee could help you fill some of your open requisitions with qualified candidates they know. Referrals are worth their weight in gold and are something you must earn, not expect. However, these referrals only come if your new hire is having a positive experience and you've stayed connected. Use auto-responders, or send automated texts or email to supplement your personal follow-up process. In addition, never underestimate the impact of sending a birthday, work anniversary, or congratulations card for a job well done. Once you have over 18 months of experience as a recruiter, 40 percent of your candidates should come from referrals. If you are an experienced recruiter and you are not obtaining referrals, this is an area that needs your attention. Referred candidates are the best candidates because there is an implied level of trust between your referral and the person who referred them. Later in this chapter we will address how to set up an effective internal employee referral program. Imagine how much easier your job would be if 40 percent of the candidates you present were referred!

It's just as important to provide nurturing when working with temporary and contract employees. If you're a third-party recruiter and the only time one of your candidates hears from you is when they get their weekly paycheck, and there is a note attached asking for referrals, chances are they will ignore your request. If you don't nurture your temporary workers or contractors, they will begin to feel all they are is a paycheck to you. When those candidates are no longer working for your current client, they have a choice whether they return to you for their next opportunity or utilize another staffing firm. The percentage of candidates you place in more than one opportunity is a great indicator of your level of nurturing. If candidates view you as their career agent, they will continue to come back to you to help them achieve both their short- and long-term career goals. Many staffing and recruiting firms have added a "candidate concierge" to their team in order to support their contractors or temporary workers and encourage redeployment. Contractors often have their next "gig" lined up three or four months before the end of their current contract. Keep in regular communication with them to ensure a strong relationship and to increase your chances of remaining their lifetime career agent.

How to build a successful employee referral program: a case study

Nancy had worked as a corporate talent acquisition professional for most of her career. She loved the profession because it allowed her to make a difference in the lives of her candidates. However, she and her team were finding it more and more difficult to attract top talent to fill many key positions. She decided to establish an employee referral program in order to help fill positions with top talent who would likely be a strong culture fit because they were recruited by current employees of the company. She also understood the relevance of on-boarding and felt employee engagement would be easier because the new hire personally knew another employee who would help make them feel welcomed and appreciated.

After spending six months creating the program, she met with the executive team to explain the details. Her plan was approved, and they announced the launch of her Employee Referral Program through the company's intranet and company bulletins to encourage participation. For lower-level positions, the referral fee was $1,000; for middle management positions, $1,500; and upper-level positions, $2,000. All referral fees paid out after six months of employment. An annual bonus of $2,500 would be paid to the person with the highest number of referrals.

Six months after launching the Employee Referral Program, Nancy realized the program was not working. The number of employee referrals had not increased, and the Human Resource Department was still struggling to keep up with the demand for top talent. She decided to survey employees to see why the program was not working. She was shocked to discover that most of the employees didn't know about it. Those individuals who were aware of the program were confused by the amount of referral fees paid for specific positions. Most of the employees didn't know whom to refer, so they didn't refer anyone. There was also confusion about how to qualify for the annual bonus. Was the award based on the number of hires or the referral fees themselves to win the $2,500? Several employees complained that they were not sure whom to contact to submit the résumés of referrals.

With this feedback, Nancy studied successful programs offered by other companies. She surveyed employees to see what would motivate them to provide referrals. Next, she changed the referral fee structure and provided training to the employees to teach them how to ask for referrals. She then published a list monthly to inform employees of jobs which were hard to fill, so they knew where to put their efforts. Nancy placed one person in charge of the program who came up with a theme of "Got Friends," published referral cards, and monitored the program. In addition to the referral fees, the referring employee was featured in the company newsletter, received a plaque and thank you notes, and had lunch with the executives of the company. The individual referring the most hires received a cash bonus, had lunch with the CEO, and was given an executive parking place for one year. These changes resulted in a dramatic increase of employee referrals who were hired, engaged, and retained and resulted in a much higher level of participation in the referral program. If your candidates are happy, engaged, and successful hires and you are not obtaining internal employee referrals, it may be time to upgrade your employee referral program.

As the example above shows, employees must clearly understand what's in it for them to participate. Once they understand how it benefits them, employees should be trained on whom to target and how to ask for referrals. The internal referral process should be as simple as possible. In addition, referral bonuses should be significant enough to cause enthusiasm and interest and should be paid on the start date, then after six months and one year. This also promotes an additional layer of nurturing from the referring employee.

Most staffing and recruiting firms show their appreciation for referrals with gift cards, referral fees, or other items which appeal to the level and profession of candidates you represent. Some firms also have a drawing at the end of the calendar year for everyone who provided referrals for a trip or other valuable gifts.

In terms of administration, your referral program should be delegated to and managed by one specific person who tracks metrics in order to identify what works and what doesn't. This person should pick a theme and survey employees to see what will motivate them to provide referrals of future employees. Lastly, recognition is the key to the success of any employee referral program. A strong employee referral program greatly enhances other talent acquisition efforts and is definitely worth the time to develop.

Summary

One area where most recruiters drop the ball is following up and nurturing the candidates they place. This is an excellent way to differentiate yourself and obtain referrals of other top talent while you build a successful employee referral program.

Key takeaways

- Your success depends on your ability to place candidates who become engaged and retained employees.

- You can help your candidates succeed by nurturing them.

- Nurturing new hires will also dramatically improve referrals of top talent.

- Align new hires before they begin their new job.

- Encourage the candidate's new supervisor or a peer to invite them to lunch during their two-week notice.

- Helping your candidate find a mentor in their new role shows your candidates you are interested in guaranteeing their success.

- Know the details of the onboarding process and fill in any gaps.

- Keep the lines of communication open to help prevent small issues from becoming major problems.

- Regularly connecting with your candidate also gives you an opportunity to ensure your candidate understands the impact of their work.

- Nurturing candidates will also benefit you by strengthening your reputation and relationship with hiring authorities.

- It is important to provide nurturing when working with temporary and contract employees as well.

- If your candidates are happy, engaged, and successful hires and you are not obtaining internal employee referrals, it may be time to upgrade your employee referral program.

- Your referral program should be delegated to and managed by one specific person who tracks metrics to identify what works and what doesn't.

Endnotes

1 Jim Dryden, "Nurturing During Preschool Years Boosts Child's Brain Growth," news release, Washington University School of Medicine in St. Louis, April 25, 2016, https://medicine.wustl.edu/news/nurturing-

preschool-years-boosts-childs-brain-growth/ (archived at https://perma.
cc/R77F-KU4A)

2 Aman Bar, "How to Prepare Your Recruiting Team for 2020," *Human Resource Executive*, December 16, 2019, https://hrexecutive.com/ how-to-prepare-your-recruiting-team-for-2020/ (archived at https:// perma.cc/HF4U-MQA3)

Create a balanced approach to recruiting

8

In previous chapters you've learned the best practices for a high-tech, high-touch approach to recruiting. However, there is one important topic we haven't directly addressed, and that topic is you! We haven't directly addressed what it takes on a personal level to be successful in the recruiting profession.

As a recruiter, one of the greatest challenges is that you have people on both sides of your process. You will often experience delays and frustrations which can make it difficult for you to stay motivated and achieve balance. Throughout my career, I've trained and managed numerous recruiters and talent acquisition professionals. I have learned that it takes a specific mindset to develop the professional skills you need to become successful as a recruiter. Some of the people I've trained went on to become very successful recruiters, but other talented hardworking recruiters struggled and ended up leaving this incredible profession.

The right mindset and having a positive attitude can help you face and overcome challenges and allow you to learn from your mistakes. Problems then become opportunities, and you will be able to effectively handle difficult hiring authorities and candidates. You will learn how to best manage your time when you have conflicting priorities and hold yourself accountable to your hiring authorities, candidates, and yourself. Lastly, you will develop the resilience that is necessary to embrace the constant change that defines this profession.

If you had told me 30 years ago that I would be in the same profession three decades later, I would have never thought that was possible. I enjoy new challenges, get bored easily, and love change. I certainly chose the perfect profession because recruiting today doesn't even resemble the profession I embraced early in my career. The workforce/workplace environments constantly change, and technology, big data, and artificial intelligence continue to escalate changes in our profession. Economic conditions, the lack of top talent worldwide, and the added challenges of engaging and retaining candidates continue to negatively affect companies. To remain successful in the recruiting profession, you must embrace and implement changes throughout your career.

It starts with your attitude

Whether you think you can, or you think you can't—you're right.
                                                        HENRY FORD

Your attitude determines your success or failure as a recruiter. This is as true when you are obtaining a job requisition as it is during aggressive hiring initiatives. Think about the last time you were given a difficult position to fill and were expected to fill it in record time. Chances are you instantly thought of the obstacles you would face. While this is common and an understandable reaction, it's not the most helpful attitude when you're responsible for filling a requisition quickly. If you tell yourself the requisition is impossible to fill and approach this challenge with a negative attitude, you may stop looking for solutions. If you start to believe you can't fill the requisition, I want you to replace the word *can't* with *won't*. Of course you can fill the requisition; the question is will you?

I've taught my children and grandchildren never to say the word *can't* as I explain to them that they are really telling me they *won't* do something. Recently, I asked my seven-year-old grandson to put away the board game we'd been playing. His instant response was "I can't," but he almost instantly looked at me and said, "I didn't mean to say

I can't because you don't like that word. Is it okay to tell you I don't want to?" This is a perfect example of how the word *can't* is synonymous for the word *won't*. If you want to elevate your level of success, take the *can't* out of your vocabulary. When you approach challenges with a positive attitude, you will become more resourceful, rather than convincing yourself you can't fill the requisition.

> The longer I live, the more I realize the impact of attitude on life. Attitude, to me, is more important than facts. It is more important than the past, than education, than money, than circumstances, than failures, than successes, than what other people think or say or do. It is more important than appearance, giftedness or skill.
>
> The remarkable thing is we have a choice every day regarding the attitude we will embrace for that day. We cannot change our past... we cannot change the fact that people will act in a certain way. We cannot change the inevitable. The only thing we can do is play on the one string we have, and that is our attitude... I am convinced that life is 10 percent what happens to me and 90 percent how I react to it. And so, it is with you... we are in charge of our attitudes. (Charles Swindoll, Founder, Insight for Living)

Your attitude can elevate your level of success from average to great. When I'm training recruiters with limited training or poor communication skills, in many instances their ultimate success or failure is determined to a great extent by their attitude and expectations. When they chose to embrace a positive attitude, they became more successful and their job satisfaction improved as well.

Your attitude is also influenced by what you watch, listen to, and read. Technology provides immediate access to information and news, but unfortunately much of the information is negative. Throughout your career, ignore negative news and ignore people who tell you that you can't accomplish something. They are entitled to their opinion, but their opinion should not define you. With a can-do attitude, you can achieve greatness in the recruiting profession. In fact, the next time you have someone tell you what you can or can't achieve, adapt the attitude "watch me" and continue to focus on your goals.

Become and stay motivated

Your overall career as a recruiter will be drastically influenced by your ability to become and stay motivated. It's easy to be motivated when things are going well, but your ability to stay motivated can be tested when you're faced with unrealistic deadlines, conflicting priorities, delays, and disappointments. Successful recruiters are resilient, motivated, and develop the mental strength to handle unpredictable issues and the challenges of the candidate-driven market. Right now, we are experiencing one of the most challenging recruiting environments in over a decade. The economy is strong, companies are desperate for talent, and there has never been a tighter candidate market worldwide. This is a recruiter's "perfect storm," but it is also when your services are needed more than ever.

How do you maintain a positive attitude in the face of such a challenging scenario? I asked successful recruiters how they stayed motivated. First, they all requested and posted testimonials and recommendations they received from both hiring authorities and candidates. When they faced challenges, reading past testimonials helped them focus on their successful track record. They also included testimonials and recommendations on their LinkedIn profile and under their email signature line. These are places where they can be seen by potential and current candidates, future and established hiring authorities, as well as recruiters themselves.

Next, they surrounded themselves with positive, encouraging people and materials. They replaced negative people and news with a supportive network of passionate, growth-oriented colleagues and friends. They also listen to or watch motivational videos, read optimistic materials, and surround themselves with motivational quotes. They often fill their work area with past awards, such as top production or personal best plaques or certificates. These items are examples of personal wins and immediately provide them with positive energy and a quick boost of confidence. However, the single most important motivating factor common to all of the successful recruiters I spoke with was their internal motivation. Why did they become a recruiter in the first place? Reflecting on why they initially became recruiters allows them to access their personal motivating factors and mental inner strength, which they frequently need to handle the unexpected issues of the recruiting profession.

When faced with unrealistic deadlines, conflicting priorities, delays, and disappointments, how do you stay motivated? What is it that helps you focus on solutions rather than obstacles? Identifying your internal motivation will enable you to view challenges as opportunities to learn, rather than obstacles to overcome. When faced with a challenge, understand what is within your control and don't spend time on things out of your control. Rather than focus on problems, immediately focus on possible solutions. When the most successful recruiters experience disappointments, they embrace a "So what, now what?" attitude and focus on what is next.

Empower yourself by choosing how you react

Earlier in this chapter the Charles Swindoll quote included: "The remarkable thing is we have a choice every day regarding the attitude we will embrace for that day." Let's take this concept one step further and discuss how you also have 100 percent control over how you choose to react. Early in my career I found myself getting upset by candidates and hiring authorities. It became obvious very quickly that getting upset was counterproductive and a waste of my valuable time and energy. Once I learned I could choose not to react to things, it was empowering. No one can upset you unless you give them permission, and why would you? When dealing with so many different people and personalities, the best decision you can often make is to decide not to react.

Make the best use of your time

Time is one of your most valuable assets, and how you spend your time directly affects what you will be able to achieve. We all have the same 168 hours each week, so why do some recruiters achieve so much, while others never seem to have enough time? The most successful recruiters understand they must focus on actions which are the best use of their time.

If you're an experienced recruiter, in order to figure out whether you are spending your time wisely, commit to conducting a time study over the next 21 working days. Write down everything you do and how often you do each specific task. After 21 days, rank the items, with 1 representing the best use of your time. Chances are the last 10 items on your list are *not* the best use of your time and, if possible, should be delegated.

The time study might suggest you eliminate or reduce some tasks you enjoy. For example, providing free consulting to candidates you know you will not place or hire is not the best use of your time. Provide alternate resources to those candidates, and focus on the candidates you will hire or place. If you are new to the recruiting profession, spend most of your time on actions which result in scheduling an interview between candidates and hiring authorities.

Manage your time by planning

If you are challenged by time management, planning is your solution. If you don't plan for success, you are inadvertently planning for failure. Without a plan, urgent issues often take the place of important, results-oriented tasks which should be your primary daily focus. When you have a plan, interruptions which demand your attention will still occur, but you will get back on track faster.

For years I would listen to speakers and experts stressing the benefits of planning. My reaction was "They're obviously not in the recruiting profession, where every phone call or email can change my priorities." As a result, I failed to plan early in my career, and it hindered my success. I decided to work with a coach who helped me plan my days, and after seeing great results, I continue to plan every single day.

If you are currently not a planner, planning 100 percent of your outgoing calls will be too much of a challenge. You may want to start by creating a list of six nonnegotiable actions—those which will help you get closest to filling a job requisition. You need to commit to completing those six actions before you leave work tomorrow. In addition, create a list of 10 outgoing calls you will make, and schedule time to make these calls in your ATS, CRM, or calendar. Doing this for 21 consecutive working days will help you develop the habit of planning. Increase the number of planned outgoing calls every month until you are planning 100 percent of them daily. This allows you to proactively control your destiny by controlling your outgoing calls versus being controlled by incoming calls.

Over time, you can begin to apply your planning skills to your personal and career development. At the end of every year, I write down 10 nonnegotiable goals in all aspects of my life which are most important, followed by five dated action items which describe the five necessary steps to achieve each goal. If the goal can't be achieved in five steps, I split the goal into two separate goals. This helps me focus on what is most important to achieve set goals.

Spend your time getting results

You obtain 80 percent of your results from 20 percent of your actions. Once you identify those activities that drive 80 percent of your results, prioritize your time and spend more time completing those exact actions. Consistently ask yourself, "Is this the best use of my time?" If your answer is no, there are three easy solutions. First, automate everything that is repetitious, template messaging, and utilize your applicant tracking system to remind you of tasks. Second, if feasible, delegate these tasks to a support person. Third, complete these tasks first thing in the morning or at the end of your day. I have the following quote taped to my computer: "Is this best use of MY time?" to remind me of how important it is to be productive versus busy. What does guarantee success is being focused on the right actions, which represent your top talents—the 20 percent of your activity that provides you with results and helps you successfully fill requisitions with the best talent.

The following are six strategies which will help you focus on results-oriented activity and fill more requisitions with the best talent who will become engaged and retained employees.

Strategy #1—Focus on scheduling more first interviews (send-outs)

The more first interviews you book, the more requisitions you will fill. I refer to the first interview as a send-out. When you are completing your planner always ask yourself, "Where is my send-out tomorrow?" You need to do whatever it takes to schedule first interviews between your candidates and hiring authorities. This is a very critical step in filling open requisitions. If you increase the number of first interviews you schedule every month, you will consistently fill more requisitions.

Strategy #2—Implement a "touch it, take action" email process

Email is one of the greatest distractions to results-oriented activities, and incoming email generally represents other people's priorities, not yours. First Step: Stop answering emails as they arrive. Instead, set aside time first thing in the morning, midday, and at the end of the day to answer email. Either respond to the email, delete it, or file it for future action. This prevents you from repeatedly reading the email in your inbox.

Email is one example of technology that can benefit you or become a major waste of your time. When you do respond to email, always change your subject line to reflect the contents of your email so you can search easily. When you obtain multiple, consistent emails from a specific source, such as Google Alerts you've set up on companies, set up a rule so these emails go directly into a designated folder and don't fill up your inbox.

After delivering a keynote address at a corporate event in Chicago, an executive walked up to me and admitted he had over 15,000 emails in his inbox. I suggested he delete all emails that were more than a year old. He admitted he never read the older email but worried he might lose important information. When he returned to his office, he instructed his administrative assistant to delete all email past six months old, and then his inbox had less than 500 emails. He called to tell me he no longer felt guilty about all the email in his inbox and that one action helped him feel and become more efficient. In the recruiting profession, you will receive hundreds of emails and need to set up rules so you never find yourself in a similar situation.

Strategy #3—Swallow the biggest frog first

Complete the activity you dread most first thing in the morning. You may not look forward to telling your hiring authority that a candidate turned down an offer or informing your candidate they did not get the job. These calls are never easy but need to be made the minute you have the information. My recruiters never wanted to tell a candidate they didn't get a job on Friday because they'd ruin their weekend. I explained that all weekend this candidate will tell everyone about the potential job offer, only to be disappointed when they receive the bad news on Monday morning. When you have information, good or bad, you need to share it.

Strategy #4—Don't drag personal issues to work

Worrying about personal issues can prevent you from peak performance. When working with hiring authorities and candidates, you should be present and focused on what's most important to them. Imagine a suitcase outside your office door, and dump all your personal issues or challenges into the suitcase before you enter your office. This will help you focus on the results-oriented activity you've planned for the day.

This same strategy should be applied to taking work issues home. Refrain from complaining about work issues once you leave the office so you can be 100 percent present and engaged in what's most important to your family when you arrive home from work.

Strategy #5—Segment your day

One of the best ways to manage your time more efficiently is to segment your day. Consider holding your incoming calls and emails from 9:00 a.m. to 12:00 p.m. each day. Set this time aside to focus on your outgoing networking calls and other top priorities. In order to recruit candidates with hard-to-find skills, you should make yourself available when they can talk openly, which is often after normal working hours. There are five and a half hours of prime time each day when you have the best chance of reaching out to prospective candidates and hiring authorities. These are the hours from 8:30 a.m. to 11:30 a.m. and 1:30 p.m. to 4:00 p.m. Plan to conduct sourcing and research around these hours. We set the time from 4:00 p.m. to 5:00 p.m. to take incoming calls from candidates who have changed their résumé or have updates on interview activity. This greatly reduces the number of incoming calls you receive from candidates who want an update.

When you are making recruiting or marketing presentations, leave this message:

> My name is _____ and my number is _____; someone suggested we talk. When you call me back, please tell whoever answers the phone to interrupt me no matter what I'm doing so I don't miss your call. I look forward to our conversation. Again, my number is _____. Have a great day. Thanks!

When you receive an incoming call and the caller states you told them to interrupt you, you now know that it is either a recruiting or a marketing hit (if you're a third-party recruiter). We tell our hiring authorities that we spend three hours daily networking for new talent for them between the hours of 9:00 a.m. and 12:00 p.m. They love the fact that we recruit daily to surface top talent.

We tell our candidates that during the day we are attempting to surface an opportunity that represents what they want to do next that will help them advance their career. This is why we set aside the time from 4:00 p.m. to 5:00 p.m. to answer incoming calls informing us of any revisions candidates have made on their résumés or updates on their additional interview activity. This will greatly reduce the number of incoming calls you receive from candidates who want an update.

When you commit to planning, understand the 80/20 rule, implement strategies that get you focused on results-oriented activity, and segment your day, you will elevate your success because you are now enjoying the benefits of knowing how to focus on the best use of your valuable time.

Balance conflicting priorities

For just a moment, put yourself in the shoes of your hiring authorities. All hiring authorities want their requisitions to be your top priority and get frustrated if you're not presenting them with top talent. If you do not have a large enough recruiting team to fill a high volume of job requisitions, you could hire contract recruiters to assist you, utilize the services of third-party recruiters, utilize offshore recruiters, or hire freelance recruiters through online resources like Upwork or Fiverr.

The good news is there are questions you can ask during your conversation or intake session with your hiring authority to establish realistic expectations and help you determine the impact of the job.

1 **What is the specific target date to fill this position?** If the target date to fill is not realistic, explain to your hiring authority the benefits of setting a later date. This is especially important when the requisition requires unique skills.

2 **Can you provide three interview times?** This helps you schedule hard-to-find talent while you have them on the phone. Often these candidates are considering multiple opportunities, which is why it benefits you to confirm an interview time. When scheduling interviews for your candidates with your hiring managers, use technology so you can confirm information with one click. Create auto-reminders to confirm scheduled interviews, and schedule a time for you to prepare both the candidate and hiring authority. To prevent no-shows or ghosting, call your candidates the morning of the interview to answer any last-minute questions. This prevents the dreaded call from your hiring authority when you're asked, "Where is your candidate?"

3 **What problems are you experiencing as a result of this job not being filled?** The answer to this question helps you to determine the urgency of each requisition. When you are juggling multiple requisitions, the jobs that are revenue-generating often receive top priority, unless the problem caused by other open jobs is determined

to be more costly. When you are planning at the end of each day, your recruiting and networking efforts should align with your top-priority requisitions. The interviews you conduct will then provide talent you can present on your top-priority business. Utilize technology to schedule and confirm interviews, but also follow up with a personal call.

If you're a third-party recruiter, job orders, contracts, or temp assignments where you have exclusivity or have been paid a retainer or engagement fee represent your top-priority business. Your next priorities are requisitions which are within your niche or where you have an established network of talent, a target date to fill, and interview times. Your last priorities should be requisitions which are given to several recruiting firms, purple squirrel requisitions, and business with clients who have such a long hiring process that you lose most of the candidates you submit.

You and your hiring authorities need to be on the same page when setting priorities. Providing them with an update on all open requisitions every Friday shows them you're working on attracting top talent, and often when you explain specific obstacles, specifications may be revised, which will usually help you fill business.

View problem areas as opportunities

Your self-esteem, motivation, and positive attitude are all tested when you're faced with problem areas. It's not a matter of *if* problems will occur; it's more a question of *when* problems will occur. You must be at your best because you're being closely scrutinized by both your candidates and clients involved.

Handling difficult hiring authorities

If you are a talent acquisition professional, you will consistently interact with your company's hiring authorities. Every hiring authority has had experience working with a recruiter. You don't know if that experience was positive or negative, and it will affect the way they interact with you. If other talent acquisition professionals or recruiters warn you about a difficult hiring authority, give them the benefit of the doubt. Often hiring authorities are difficult because they're under pressure to meet deadlines and realize they don't have the team they need. When you help alleviate their hiring issues, you can develop a rapport that leads to trust and a great working relationship.

One way to start off your working relationship on a positive note is to provide your hiring authorities with a list of written expectations. When you quickly change your focus from the problem to possible solutions, you will enjoy better results. When hiring authorities review your sourcing, recruiting, screening, interviewing, and presentation process, they understand the work you will do on their behalf. Providing written expectations will also help individuals who are brand new to the hiring process.

Write down what they can expect from you along with a list of what you need from them to be effective. For example, when you request interview times and a target date to hire, explain that it helps you to know when to begin your recruiting process. I've found that when you ask the parties involved for their solution, they often provide a solution far easier than the one you were contemplating. Be sure to mention that you will call them every Friday afternoon to provide them with an update on their open requisitions, so they understand how it benefits them to take your call. When they hear what you've experienced, they are often much more willing to alter their specifications to eliminate some of the obstacles.

If you're a third-party recruiter, your income is based on your ability to fill the business you write. If there is a lack of rapport or trust with a client, you may consider giving the business to another recruiter. If you've worked on several searches with no hires, you could either walk away or request a retainer or engagement fee before working on another position.

Handling difficult candidates

When candidates are difficult or reject you, often they don't understand how you can benefit them. It's important to recognize that they are not rejecting you personally; they are rejecting what you're saying. Most individuals who are working are open to listen to an opportunity that could represent their next logical career move. If you focus on what is most important to each candidate, you will be more successful in recruiting top talent.

At the same time there are candidates who don't respect recruiters or will use your job opportunity as a way to obtain a counteroffer from their current employer. This can be a frustrating waste of your time. If a candidate is difficult from your first contact, doesn't show up for interviews, or won't give you the information you need to properly represent them, walk away. Their behavior will only get worse as they progress through your process, and rarely will they become a successful hire. Invest your time and efforts in candidates with whom you've been able to develop rapport and trust.

Hold yourself accountable

Key performance indicators and ratios

To achieve a balanced approach to recruiting you need to understand the key performance indicators (KPIs) that recruiters use to measure their success. One commonly used KPI is the individual ratios which are influenced by your attitude, expertise, experience, established network, passion, and tenacity. As you improve your sourcing, recruiting, interviewing, and matching abilities, your ratios will decrease because you know whom and how to call. Your ratios show you exactly what results are needed daily in order for you to attain or surpass your goals.

Let me provide you with an example. If you schedule three interviews before someone is hired and you need two hires per week, you need to schedule six interviews with your hiring managers per week. Next you need to know how many candidates you screened before you set up an interview with your hiring authorities. If you screened three candidates before scheduling an interview with your hiring authority, then you need to conduct 18 interviews per week or three or four per day. This takes the guesswork out of where to place your focus.

The positive impact of a weekly review

To achieve balance with conflicting priorities, interruptions, problems, and people on both sides of your process, there is something you *can* do to stay on track and hold yourself accountable. Block off 30 minutes between 4:00 p.m. and 4:30 p.m. as a recurring event for every Friday on your calendar. You are going to step back and review your past week, as if you were hired as an outside consultant.

Ask yourself three questions during this review:

1 "What did I do right?" In other words, what actions provided 80 percent of your results? Commit to doing more of those exact actions in the following week.

2 "How did I waste my time?" Did you interview candidates you're never going to hire or place? Did you read the same email repeatedly? Commit to stop doing those things immediately.

3 "What new idea am I implementing this month to improve my results?" Hopefully, you're implementing ideas shared in this book.

When you review your progress weekly, you may have a bad week, but you will never have a bad month or quarter. This allows you to hold yourself accountable on a weekly basis and encourages you to consistently implement new ideas every month.

It takes 21 days of consistent repetition to replace an old ineffective habit with a new habit. If you attempt to implement too many new ideas, often you will end up implementing nothing. If you implement one new idea every month, you will enjoy improved results.

Add unattained goals to future months (for third-party recruiters)

Another key strategy to hold yourself accountable is to never erase a production goal. If there is ever a month where you do not attain your goals, calculate the difference between your goal and what you achieved. Divide the total by the remaining months in the year, and add the number to those months. This greatly enhances your ability to consistently achieve your goals.

Embrace change

Change is the only constant.

Heraclitus

Recruiting is a profession dependent on the changes made by individual candidates and hiring authorities. Why would companies need recruiters if no one ever left their jobs? Why would candidates seek out the assistance of a recruiter if they were content to stay with their current company until they retired?

Since clients and candidates are the basis of your business, it is important to keep yourself informed of what is happening in their companies and lives. Make it a point to read the business and trade publications they read. Listen for changes and trends during your discussions with them. It's a great idea to join the professional association which represents the industry or profession that you work in so you can stay informed on anticipated trends.

In addition to being dependent on the changes incurred by other industries, the recruiting industry itself is subject to changes relating to the demographics of the workplace as well as advances in technology. Each day 10,000 Baby Boomer employees are retiring and 10,000 Millennial and Generation Z employees are entering and progressing throughout the workforce. In fact, in January 2020, Millennials represented over 50 percent of the workforce, and by 2025, they will represented 75 percent of the workforce. This changes how and where recruiters will seek out the best talent. If you want to attract tech-savvy talent from the Millennials and Generation Z, you will need to meet that talent on the platforms and in the digital spaces where they are spending their time.

In addition, advances in technology have led to the automation of many tasks that were formerly handled by people. This has led to the creation of "gig" employment, which impacts what it even means to be an employee. Many companies are embracing a new workforce model in which full-time direct hires—who are full-time salaried employees—are working together with flexible or contract employees in order to get work done. Employers can scale up for a major project quickly when they utilize contract employees and can reduce their workforce just as rapidly. They have also realized that retention improves when they surround their core employees with contractors. Contractors often have specialized skills which are needed for a specific project and support the work done by the core employees.

In 2020, for the first time in history, over 50 percent of the workforce in the US will not be working the traditional 40-hour work week. More candidates than ever before will choose to work as a contractor, independent contractor, temporary worker, virtual employee, or be self-employed, work for a company like Upwork or Fiverr, or have other alternative work arrangements. This trend has an impact on who will be hiring recruiters. Companies need to determine if they should hire internal talent acquisition professionals, third-party recruiters, contract recruiters, or utilize an offshore team. This trend also impacts where recruiters will look for candidates. You either anticipate trends and adapt to change, or your competition will run right over you. You can't continue to do things the same way and expect better results. It's also important to adapt to the latest technology and make adjustments that take you out of your comfort zone, which proves you are growing throughout your career as a recruiter.

High-tech tools are a critical part of your recruiting process but must be combined with personal contacts to add the high-touch element. Automated tools can source candidates, administer assessments, schedule interviews, and provide updates to candidates. In Canada, McDonald's was the first brand to use the social media platform Snapchat when they launched "Snapplications," a one-day virtual hiring event which allowed job seekers to instantly apply for jobs at McDonald's directly through the Snapchat app.

As useful and efficient as it is, technology is ultimately a tool which should support and enhance human interaction. The quality of the relationship a candidate has with their recruiter and hiring authority determines if they have a positive or negative candidate experience. The appropriate use of technology combined with a high-touch recruiting relationship will improve the long-term quality of the talent you represent. This will most definitely enhance your success as a recruiter.

Summary

One of the most important assets in the recruiting, interviewing, and hiring process is you. This chapter addressed many of the challenges you face and how to handle them using a high-tech, high-touch approach to recruiting.

You learned how to balance conflicting priorities, handle difficult candidates and clients, effectively overcome objections from hiring authorities, and solve problem areas. You then learned how technology will continue to impact recruiting and why you must embrace change throughout your career.

To attain great success in the recruiting profession, it takes the right mindset and a positive attitude. It's important to view problems as opportunities to effectively handle difficult hiring authorities or candidates. When faced with conflicting priorities, you need to manage your time effectively in order to hold yourself accountable to your hiring authorities, candidates, and yourself. In addition, you will develop the resilience necessary to embrace the constant change and trends that define the recruiting profession.

Key takeaways

- Keeping a positive attitude is critical to your success as a recruiter.
- Managing your time requires planning.
- Planning is the solution to time management.
- If you are new to planning, commit to completing six top priorities for 21 days.
- Determine what 20 percent of your activities drive 80 percent of your results.
- Scheduling more interviews is critical to filling job requisitions.
- Review your email and take appropriate action no more than three times a day.

- Complete the activity that you consider the most difficult first so you can be more productive.
- Be present with candidates and clients when you are working.
- Segment your time in order to achieve more.
- Effectively prioritize searches by the impact of the job.
- Prioritize interviews to align with the hottest requisitions.

Selling your services as a third-party recruiter

9

The need for utilizing third-party recruiters is increasing due to the candidate-driven market, global competition for talent, and the additional challenges of hiring candidates who become engaged and retained employees and don't end up as costly turnover statistics. Companies realize recruiters have established networks of passive candidates who are not reading website postings or job board ads. Most recruiting firms specialize in a specific industry or niche, and clients prefer to work with recruiters who specialize in the exact type of talent they hire. In fact, companies with their own talent acquisition team often hire an outside firm to help them fill specialized roles as well as temporary or contract positions. Unlike in-house recruiters, third-party recruiters are dependent on their ability to target and contract with the best clients who will hire them to fill their open positions with the best talent. As a result, success as a third-party recruiter involves attracting and retaining the best clients and candidates and developing a long-term relationship with both. In other words, success as a third-party recruiter requires a high-tech, high-touch approach.

In this chapter, I will reveal the tremendous impact the clients you represent will have on your income, reputation, and level of success you attain. You will learn how to identify your area of specialization, conduct revenue modeling, change the perception of third-party recruiters, differentiate yourself from your competition, explain the benefits in utilizing your services, overcome objections, understand why you need to consistently upgrade your clients, and lastly, prove the return on investment of utilizing your services.

If you are an in-house corporate recruiter transitioning into third-party recruiting, you must now learn how to attract the best clients. You do not have hiring authorities that must automatically utilize your services, as you did when you were an in-house recruiter. Add your personality to the scripts we've provided, and take time to learn how to overcome the client objections that we address later in this chapter.

If you are new to the third-party recruiting profession and do not work for an established staffing and recruiting firm, you will need to determine which industry or niche will become your area of specialization. Ideally, you want to be recruiting in areas where there is a high demand and low supply of talent. Start by reviewing articles, job board ads, website postings, and media coverage of the fastest-growing professions. This reveals where your ability to provide top talent will have the greatest value.

Specializing in a niche is a marketable differentiator to clients and candidates because it allows you to position yourself as an expert. If you choose to specialize in the food service industry or place HR professionals in all industries, your goal is to become the top expert in your niche with the best network of talent and clients. As a result, clients are more likely to pay full fees or higher margins, and candidates will want access to your clients, who represent the most preferred companies.

If you are a third-party recruiter working with an established recruiting firm, you will want to conduct revenue modeling on an annual basis to ensure the effectiveness of your recruiting. You and your manager should review the industry, job title, location, time to hire, profit margin, and retention of candidates your firm has placed over the last two years. Technology and your applicant tracking system will assist you in compiling this information. By studying the fills (temp/contract) and placements (direct hires) that successfully closed in the past 18 to 24 months, you can determine where and how to focus your efforts. You will also want to reach out to past clients who are inactive and conduct research to identify companies that are actively recruiting that you will want to target as potential clients.

When you're reaching out to prospects, it's important to sound like you are familiar with their industry, which is why educating yourself on industry trends and statistics is important. You might seek out the professional association and read their website and publications for trends, leads, and verbiage to help you sound like an insider. Many associations also publish their membership list, which could help you identify additional prospects. You'll also want to attend any functions that will allow you to meet your prospects. If possible, join a professional association as an affiliate member and volunteer to help on the membership committee, which could yield prospective clients for you.

Once you feel comfortable enough to begin reaching out to client prospects, you will need to identify the correct contact within each of your targeted companies. This can differ greatly from company to company depending on the level of job and size of your prospect. Technology has made it easy to research hiring authorities before you reach out. Never underestimate the power of talking directly to hiring authorities who may have a weak link in their department but haven't updated their job requisition or informed their Human Resources department.

It's important to realize that most prospects have had an experience working with a third-party recruiter. They may have used a recruiter in the past as a candidate and were not placed in a job, or they have used the services of a recruiter to fill open requisitions and were not satisfied with the results. It's important for you to understand the following perceptions that may exist but, more importantly, what you can do to change these perceptions. I don't agree with most of these perceptions, but my opinion isn't important. If your prospective clients have any of these perceptions, that is their reality. However, if you follow the suggestions provided, you will eliminate these perceptions.

Potential clients may believe that third-party recruiters:

- **Know nothing about our business before contacting us.** With the abundance of information online, there is no excuse for making an uninformed cold call. It's easy to set up Google Alerts for each prospect, review their website, read press and media, and connect with past and current employees on LinkedIn. It's also important to review the LinkedIn profile of the person you intend to contact.

  A perfect example of recruiters conducting no research is something my company experiences every January. The name of our firm is HR Search (not H&R Block). Every January we receive calls from recruiters who are marketing candidates who have experience in tax return preparation. When we inform them we are a search firm, they continue to market the candidate, proving to us that they are not prepared and are not listening. When you make informed client development calls, you will differentiate yourself from your competition.

- **Bombard us with calls from job board ads.** This is the number one complaint I hear when I'm speaking to audiences of hiring authorities or talent acquisition professionals. The question they ask is "Why would I utilize a third-party recruiter when I've just spent thousands of dollars on job board ads?" Your prospective clients prefer to work with a recruiter who has targeted them as ideal clients. These recruiters share their personal brand and differentiators, and explain the benefits in utilizing their services. They don't only target companies that have just run a job board ad.

- **Don't represent candidates we can find ourselves on job boards.** Companies are spending billions of dollars on job board ads. They don't want you to present the same candidates they are attracting. They expect you to present passive candidates; these are individuals who are working, have a track record of success, and represent 85 percent of the talent pool. Clients often ask the question "When did recruiters stop recruiting?" It's important to build your network of passive candidates whom your clients prefer to hire.

- **Disappear when problems occur.** When problems occur, you should be at your best, but that's not the perception of many hiring authorities. Focus on possible solutions rather than dwelling on the problem. It's a good practice to ask your hiring authority for their solution. Often you will be surprised how simple it is to solve basic problems. When issues are not easily resolved, your clients will closely scrutinize your actions. Suggest solutions that not only solve the problem but "wow" your client as well.

  After a flight delay, I got to my hotel after midnight and was informed there were no rooms with a king-size bed or bathtub, as I had requested. They offered me a cup of coffee, and I declined because I am a tea drinker. As I was unpacking, the hotel delivered a pot of hot tea and an assortment of cheese, fruit, and crackers with a note apologizing for the mix-up. I wrote to the general manager of the hotel and gave an exceptional rating online. This is an example of how to "wow" a client.

- **Don't take time to understand our challenges.** Clients will buy your services but don't like to be sold, especially when you pitch your services too soon. Refrain from selling anything until you understand your prospect's challenge. This is the only way you can position yourself as the logical solution.

- **Become defensive if we disagree with them.** As a result of this perception, when a client screens out a candidate, the only feedback they provide is "Your candidate was not a fit." This does not help you fine-tune your search. You can resolve this by asking your clients, "What was my candidate missing? I don't want to waste your time and would like to fine-tune my recruiting efforts on your behalf."

- **Assume we are all the same.** If you've ever been referred to as "you people," chances are this client feels that all third-party recruiters are identical. It's your personal brand, which is your track record of success, that will differentiate you and help you land the best clients.

- **Can't overcome simple objections.** Prospective clients have shared that they know the two or three objections they can use to get 95 percent of third-party recruiters off the phone. They are also amazed that they never hear from the recruiter again and wonder how badly the recruiter wanted their business. Later in this chapter we will provide you with the top objections you will receive from prospects, with responses to overcome the objections. If you become great at overcoming objections, you will change the perceptions of prospective clients.

- **Can't be trusted to tell the truth.** This is the perception that upsets me the most. We have a moral and ethical responsibility to tell the truth, so we can develop a rapport with our clients based on trust. Your actions will prove to your clients that you are honest and can be trusted.

- **Are one of many vendors we utilize.** When you first work with a new client, you are perceived as a vendor. When your client sees the caliber of talent you present and successfully hires from you, you will then elevate the working relationship to trusted advisor and consultant.

Setting up your client development process

Selling to new prospects is a process. It's important to follow a proven, predictable sales process with allowances for your personality and selling style. It may take some time to make the first contact and establish a connection, so reach out to prospects six times in the first nine weeks to gain name recognition, making sure you record every outreach effort in your applicant tracking system. I'd suggest mixing up your approach through a combination of calls, emails, texts, and information sent by direct mail. During conversations with prospects, ask what competitors your prospective client respects or the type of talent that is the most challenging for them to hire. Marketing a candidate from one of their competitors or hard-to-find talent is a very effective way to schedule interviews with a new client.

Whenever possible, schedule a face-to-face meeting with prospects so you can begin to develop rapport, identify and understand their priorities, and experience the company culture. Because hiring authorities change jobs often, it's important to develop multiple contacts within each client. It takes determination, focus, and tenacity to develop clients, and you don't want to lose a client if you lose your contact.

How to reach out to prospects

When you are reaching out to prospective clients, you only have a few seconds to make an impression. Every recruiter says they're different, but when asked how, most say the same things. There are a few things you can do to differentiate yourself and attract new clients.

1 **Ask questions.** You don't want to sound like a rookie recruiter by asking "Do you have any current job opening I could help you with?" The greatest mistake made by most recruiters is that they try to sell their services too quickly. Differentiate yourself by asking the client about their problems before you start to sell. Ask open-ended questions that will provide you with information that reveals this prospect's hiring challenges.

2 **Position yourself as an expert.** You need to be well read so you can anticipate trends that will affect your client base. Technology continues to change at an accelerated pace, and your hiring authorities want to know how it will affect their industry or profession, changes they need to make, and how technology will impact them as well as their employees in the future.

3 **Share your track record.** The one thing your competitors don't have is your track record of success. Potential clients will review your LinkedIn profile to see your accomplishments and the impact they have had on other hiring authorities. If you've helped other hiring authorities successfully hire and retain top talent, share these stories both on your LinkedIn profile and in your pitch. If you're a new recruiter, you could share the track record of your team until you establish one.

4 Provide a list of client expectations. Prospects are often confused about what to expect from a recruiter because the sales and client development process can differ greatly from one recruiter to another. To eliminate confusion, provide your prospects with a written list of expectations. Outline what they can expect from you and what you need from them in order to recruit the caliber of talent they will hire without hesitation. I have provided a sample of what a client expectations document might look like in the online resource guide that accompanies this book.

Now that you have an idea of how you can differentiate yourself, it's time to start reaching out to your prospects. Below are four sample scripts that I have successfully used in my own client development efforts. You'll want to tailor these scripts to make sure they sound like you and reflect your personal brand and style.

Script 1: Rather than asking your prospect if they'd like to meet with you (which gives them the opportunity to say no), skip a step and start the conversation by immediately having them focus on what kind of presentation you could deliver that would best meet their needs.
"In order to better acquaint myself with what is important to you, I would like to meet with you personally to discuss your staffing needs. What kind of presentation do you prefer?"
The most common response is "Whatever type of presentation you would normally do," which means you've been successful in scheduling your initial client visit.

Script 2: Use the research you've done on their open positions to ask questions about how you might help. When you uncover their concerns or problems, you know where to focus your efforts and can position yourself as a solution.
"I understand that you are currently having staffing needs in the following areas (list the positions). Are there any concerns or problems you're experiencing that I may assist you with?"

Script 3: This prospect has likely been approached by other recruiters, so distinguish yourself by not trying to "sell" right away. Get them to talk about what is most important to them, and use this information to better meet their expectations.

"When you hire a staffing company to help identify top talent for your company, what is most important to you?"

Script 4: If you get the impression that the prospect doesn't have any open positions right now, reveal how you can help them in the future. Their response to this question will help you tailor the candidates you market to this prospect.

"When you think about the future of your company, what type of talent will represent your greatest hiring challenge? When I come across individuals with those credentials, would you like to hear from me?"

Overcoming client objections

Once you begin reaching out to prospects, you will hear objections. If you are not overcoming objections, you are making customer service calls, not sales calls. Client development does not provide instant gratification. It is a relationship-building process that takes time and effort. Rather than getting discouraged by objections, view them as a request for more information or a possible desire to engage your services. After all, if they really were not interested, they would simply hang up!

Below I've outlined the most common objections and some suggested responses to help you effectively overcome them.

"We don't use third-party recruiters."

Clients have learned that this objection is a very effective way to end most sales calls. However, you can try to keep the conversation going by asking open-ended questions that identify issues or problems this prospect is experiencing. You can then position your services as the solution. For example, you might ask:

- "What jobs are the most challenging for you to fill?"
- "How much of your time is spent attempting to fill the hard-to-fill positions?"

- "When you look at the next 12 months, which candidates would be the most difficult for you to attract?"
- "It would greatly enhance your ability to attract top talent if you utilized our services. Could you tell me who makes that decision?"
- "May I use your name when I contact this person?"

"Our company is cutting back and not hiring."

This objection is an effective way to postpone utilizing your services. You can respond with:

- "Many of our clients are cutting their marginal employees while they continue to hire specialized top talent. What is your most difficult talent to attract?"
- "Do you have any upcoming projects that will require specialized talent or temporary/contract talent? We have access to outstanding contractors."

"Our approved vendors fill all our positions."

Many recruiters will hang up after hearing that the company already has an approved vendor. And clients often don't want to go through the hassle of getting a new vendor approved. Don't give up that easily! Instead, respond with:

- "When I first contacted my top clients, they said the same thing to me, and I earned my way to become their top resource for top talent. I'd like the opportunity to do the same for you."
- "Our goal is to become your trusted advisor, but we realize the first step is to become an approved vendor. What steps do we need to take?"
- "We specialize in and represent an outstanding network of top talent. Do you have any hard-to-fill positions we might be able to help you with?"
- "Would it benefit your company if you could hire from an additional recruiter for projects requiring specialized hard-to-find skills?"

"We don't have any current open requisitions."

While they may not have any requisitions at the time, they may not realize that you can proactively present top talent if you understand their priorities and future needs. A few great responses are:

- "Is there a talent or skill missing in your department?"
- "When you look into the future, what is going to be your greatest hiring challenge?"
- "Do you know of anyone else in your industry who is hiring?"
- "Is there someone you've hired that you'd like to upgrade?"
- "If you are not hiring contractors, you could be overstaffed."

"Send me some résumés."

Never send a résumé or CV with contact information until you understand their needs.

- "In order for me to send you an appropriate résumé or CV that will not waste your time, I would need a thorough understanding of your open jobs."

"Can you give me an extended guarantee?"

Recruitment guarantees keep the recruiter engaged with the candidate even after they have started in their new role. Essentially, these guarantees hold the recruiter responsible if the candidate they presented decides to leave before the end of the guarantee period. While a 90-day guarantee is the industry standard, clients may ask for an extended guarantee. Here are some ways to address this question:

- "Most of the individuals we represent are working and have a successful track record. With their proven record of success, you should be able to determine if your decision to hire them was correct within a relatively short period of time."
- "Your contractor will be working for you, which is a working interview. You have the opportunity to watch the person work before you convert them to a direct hire."

"Am I on some list? I've heard from three recruiting firms this week."

If your target industry is experiencing rapid growth and change, chances are your client has been approached by all of your competitors who are building their businesses. You can differentiate yourself from your competitors by responding with:

- "We represent the best talent in your industry and also want to represent the best companies. This is really a compliment to both you and your company."

- "I've actually targeted your company as one I'd like to represent for the following reasons: (share information you've researched)."

- "Is there a difficult requisition you're trying to fill that could be a test of our ability to attract the best talent for your company?"

"We are already paying for job boards."

Companies are spending billions of dollars on job board ads. However, job boards target only the 15 percent of all eligible candidates who are currently looking for a new job. As a recruiter, your focus should be on those passive candidates—the 85 percent of qualified candidates who are not actively looking. Here's how you can respond to show how you can add value as their recruiter:

- "Do you realize you're limiting yourself to only individuals who are actively looking for a job? This approach limits your reach to only candidates who are reading the job boards."

- "We have a network of outstanding candidates who are not on the job boards. They represent some of the best talent available."

- "Would you like access to people who are working, successful, not in an active search but would listen to the right opportunity? We can provide access to this hidden market of candidates."

- "We don't utilize job boards. Would it be a good decision to have comparison candidates to enable you to hire the top talent available versus the talent conducting an active search?"

Each time you encounter a new objection, write it down and role-play possible ways to overcome the objection. You don't want the same objection to prevent you from attaining the level of success you deserve.

Writing fillable business

Now that you've overcome your prospect's objections and converted them into a client, you need to ensure that you can realistically meet their expectations. Too often recruiters accept a job order and then hang up the phone and say, "What a ridiculous order! We're not going to work on this because we'll never fill it!" Your success is not dependent on the number of job orders, contracts, or temp assignments you write, but on the business you successfully fill with top talent.

Clients often ask for the impossible—what is known in the recruiting profession as a "purple squirrel," or a candidate so perfectly suited for a role that they are unlikely to even exist. To prevent unrealistic expectations, you and your client should agree on the specifications of their job order, contract, or temp assignment. If they ask for the impossible, explain to them what specifications need to be adjusted or eliminated for you to fill the position. This helps position you as a workforce/workplace expert and can differentiate you from competitors who may write the business but not recruit for it or provide any results.

The 12 criteria for "fillable" business include:

1 **The opportunity is within your area of specialization.** You need to mirror past placements or fills by staying within your area of specialization. If you don't, you cannot multi-use the candidate or the clients.

2 **The hiring authority is willing to give you details.** If the hiring authority does not provide you with details up front, chances are this person will not give you feedback about candidates submitted or interviews. Always explain the "what's in it for me" (WIIFM) to the client. Make it clear how they benefit from providing you with a detailed job description, including performance objectives, for each position.

3 There is a clear understanding of the opportunity. Make sure you are clear on the job opportunity before you begin your recruiting efforts. To ensure your understanding, ask your client if the first recruiting presentation can be made to them. When your client hears how you are presenting their company and opportunity, they almost always add additional information that can help you improve your recruiting presentations.

4 The client is willing to give you their targeted date to fill this position. Ask for a specific target date for filling the position. Never accept the answers ASAP, immediately, or yesterday. Timing is critical to you, your candidate, and your client, if you want to fill business written.

5 You have determined that they are experiencing pain by this position not being filled. If there is no pain, there is no urgency to fill this position. If the position is currently being filled by someone else and the company can avoid an additional salary, most employers will avoid bringing on additional staff until it causes a problem.

6 The interviewing process is reasonable. The best candidates are likely being approached by other recruiters or have found other job opportunities on their own. Make this clear to your hiring authority in order to keep the process moving.

7 The client understands the importance of feedback, and they communicate with you. Feedback helps you fine-tune your search efforts and gives your candidates vital information for their future interviewing efforts. The easiest way to obtain feedback is to ask your client what was missing from the candidate they interviewed, explaining you don't want to waste their time.

8 The salary level is commensurate with the experience required. Review the past positions that were filled and research salary surveys to determine if the money offered is commensurate with the required experience level. If you are recruiting in the US, be aware that many states have passed salary ban laws, which prevent you from asking a candidate what they are currently earning. You can, however, ask what salary range they would consider.

9 You have a detailed copy of their benefit package. The right benefits package can mean the difference between success or failure in placing a candidate. You must know what benefits your candidate currently has and the costs involved, so you can compare them to the benefits offered by your client. Even if your client is offering a high salary level, benefits can cause a candidate to turn down an offer.

10 This is one of your targeted companies. If this is not one of your targeted companies, make sure this company meets the criteria you have set for your profitable territory and is a company that has been identified as most desirable by candidates interviewed. When the market is candidate-driven, you can't afford to represent companies with a bad reputation.

11 You're able to establish rapport with your contact. Rapport is established as trust is earned. You don't have to like your clients, but you do have to be able to establish a rapport that will lead to trust.

12 You have interviewing times. When you receive a commitment from your client to interview, you make a commitment to surface talent. I can't tell you the number of times a recruiter writes an order, recruits on the order, has other recruiters submit candidates, and then the client disappears off the face of the earth. Your job is to book send-outs, and when you request interviewing times up front, send-outs are guaranteed. My definition of a send-out is a first interview between your candidate and client.

At the end of the day, it hurts your reputation to accept orders that you won't be able to fill. Make sure you are representing the companies most attractive to your prospective candidates and are writing business that you know your recruiters can fill. Send a copy of the plan to everyone in the hiring process to make sure they are all on the same page. I find that even in my business, we still encounter many changes with long-term clients, especially from their direct report. Begin every subsequent conversation with "Has anything changed since the last time we talked?," and schedule a call every Friday to provide updates on all active job orders, contracts, or temporary work assignments.

Offer pricing options

The best way to earn money in recruiting is to develop a high-tech, high-touch approach in which you not only present the best talent to your clients, but you also become their hiring consultant. They trust you to help them discover and fill their most important positions on a consistent basis.

If you are just starting out or are recruiting in a new industry, you may not have an established track record with any clients yet, so you may need to negotiate your fees with clients. Pricing options are determined by the level of search, client expectations, and how clients want to pay for services. The four primary pricing options are shown in Table 9.1. How a client pays you will often drive your recruitment efforts.

For example, if a client wants ownership of candidates presented until they have eliminated them from consideration, they must pay for either a retained search or some type of engagement or container which is a mix between contingency and retained. If a client wants to motivate and incentivize a contingent recruiter to work a difficult search, they often are willing to pay retainers, partial retainers, engagement fees, hours worked, per candidate, or increase fee percentages. So often, it is client payment issues that drive recruitment models.

Table 9.1 Four primary pricing options

Type of search	Compensated when
Contingency search	Candidate is hired
Retained search	1/3 up front
	1/3 after 30 days or predetermined number of candidates are submitted
	1/3 upon successful hire
Engagement/container	Predetermined percentage is paid up front
Contract/temp	Pay rate is normally paid weekly

Contingency

When a client prefers to pay after results are provided, they often opt to work with a recruiter on a contingency arrangement. These are not exclusive searches, and the client will often utilize multiple recruiting firms to provide talent. In addition, the client continues to conduct their internal search. These positions are normally under the $150,000 range.

When a recruiter is working a contingent search, they do not reveal the name of their client until the candidate has expressed an interest in the opportunity. However, the names of all candidates recruited for a specific search are also not shared with the client. The candidate presented to the client is often marketed to other companies, because there is no exclusivity in this type of arrangement. Most contingent recruiters will provide a Friday update on their progress, but there is not an abundance of written updates and reports. In contingency, the recruiter is not compensated until the job is successfully filled and the invoice is paid by the client.

Retained search

When clients have a C-suite position or high-impact opportunity, clients often opt to identify a retained search firm that specializes in their industry or niche, to conduct a retained search.

The client partially invests before results are provided, usually paying one-third of the fee up front, one-third after a predetermined number of qualified candidates are presented, and the last one-third after a successful hire. If the retained search recruiter does not fill the position, they are not paid the last one-third of the fee.

Retained search recruiters share the name of their client to help attract top talent. There is no fear of competition, because they have exclusivity with this client. Detailed documentation is provided to the client throughout the retained search process, including the names of every candidate surfaced. The client has exclusive rights to those candidates until they eliminate them from consideration. Depending on the retained search agreement, additional costs involved during the retained search process are often billed to the client. The retained search recruiter is paid as payments are received from the client.

Engagement/container

Engaged search is a hybrid model between contingency and retained search in which a percentage of the fee is paid when the search begins. The remainder of the fee is only paid if a candidate is hired. Before you consider working on an opportunity with an engagement or container option, you must qualify the order up front. You must also be ready to overcome objections or hesitations clients may have about paying any money up front, stressing the benefits they will enjoy.

Temp/contract

Many employers hire outside recruiters to complement their core employees. They realize that if they are not utilizing temps or contractors, they are likely overstaffed. The assignment or contract is a working interview that often leads to a direct hire.

Elevate your client relationship

As with candidates, your success as a third-party recruiter is dependent on your ability to nurture your client relationships. Hiring authorities will stop using your services if they don't feel that you make them a priority. You also need to regularly provide feedback and the results of your efforts. If the candidates you place do not become engaged or retained employees, your clients will seek out the services of your competitors.

Summary

This chapter helped you identify the best companies to target, showed you how to differentiate yourself, and showed you how to overcome objections. You also learned how to write fillable business and elevate the relationship you have with your clients. As a result, you will attract the clients who can provide you with the greatest level of success.

Key takeaways

- Most recruiting firms specialize in a specific industry or niche, and clients prefer to work with recruiters who specialize in the exact type of talent they hire.

- It's important to understand the perception of some prospective clients so you can learn to improve them.

- By studying the fills (temp/contract) and placements (direct hires) that successfully closed across all industries in the past 18 to 24 months, you can calculate the amount of recruiting business done within each industry or profession and choose the niche and titles which look the most promising for you.

- Because hiring authorities change jobs often, you want to develop multiple contacts within each client. You don't want to lose a client if you lose your contact.

- Differentiate yourself from your competition by focusing on your accomplishments, asking questions, providing a list of client expectations, and positioning yourself as a hiring expert.

- If you're not facing objections in working with clients, you're not conducting a sales call.

- View objections as requests for more information or a desire to engage your services.

- It hurts your reputation to accept orders that you won't be able to fill.

- Make sure you are representing the companies most attractive to your prospective candidates and are writing business that you know your recruiters can fill.

- Pricing options are determined by the level of search, client expectations, and how clients want to pay for services. How a client pays you will often drive your recruitment efforts.

- The best way to earn money in recruiting is to develop a high-tech, high-touch approach in which you not only present the best talent to your clients, but you also become their hiring consultant.

- Retained search is the higher-end service in pricing models and mandates dedicated time and superior expertise in your niche.

- Many employers hire outside recruiters to complement their core employees.

Conclusion

First, I want to congratulate you for choosing the recruiting profession, where you can daily change people's lives for the better. I want to thank you for reading my book, and I'm thrilled that you now understand how everyone benefits by a high-tech, high-touch approach to recruiting. You're also equipped with new techniques that will help you positively impact even more candidates and hiring authorities, as you continue to fine-tune your skills.

You've learned what changes in the hiring process can enhance your ability to get the best talent hired. More of your candidates will be screened in because you now understand the value of obtaining performance objection versus writing a skills-based job requisition. I think you'll be amazed the next time you write a skills-based job requisition and request performance objectives from your hiring authorities.

When you ask the question "How will this candidate be evaluated as a success in 6 or 12 months. What would they have to achieve?," you will observe the disconnect between the traditional laundry list of skills and what your candidate really needs to achieve in order to be deemed successful. I predict you will schedule more interviews for qualified candidates who will become successful, engaged, and retained employees.

This should also end your frustration with having qualified candidates screened out because they don't have one of nine skills listed on a traditional job requisition. If someone has accomplished a similar objective, maybe on a lesser scale, you know they will succeed. This is a real game changer, but you must explain to your hiring authorities how obtaining performance objectives benefits them.

You've also learned the importance of communicating differently. Rather than communicating only by texts, email, and voicemail, you now know candidates will talk to you when they understand how you can benefit their career growth. Ask yourself if you're the one who is more comfortable texting or sending an email. Set a goal to have an actual conversation during every third contact with either your candidates or hiring authorities, and your ability to have productive conversations will dramatically increase.

To fill your requisitions faster, you can utilize scripts provided to proactively recruit 85 percent of the talent pool. This is more effective than posting and praying, which gives you access only to 15 percent and is more expensive. You can now build a network of top talent in advance of need, and these candidates will not be represented by 10 other recruiters because they are not conducting an active job search. A candidate-driven market is where your services are needed most, and becoming a proactive recruiter will help you fill job requisitions faster.

You've probably always been an effective communicator, but now you have additional insightful questions to ask. But, before you utilize the questions, I want to ask you a very important question. As a result of reading this book, are you listening more effectively?

You've learned to listen to understand where a person is coming from and see the world through their eyes, which will enable you to do a better job for them. You also know it's not your job to agree or disagree with candidates or hiring authorities, but to determine what opportunity they will accept or person they will hire without hesitation.

Just imagine the impact when you target the 85 percent of the talent pool who are not reading website postings or job board ads. You've learned to proactively recruit this talent, and they are often the candidates who have the DNA of the peak performers who are most desired by your hiring authorities. This approach may take you out of your comfort zone, which is why I suggest you utilize the scripts provided and then just add your wonderful personality.

The high-tech, high-touch approach also improves the hiring process and how candidates are screened in or out, removing emotion and bias. The next time you lose a great candidate because the hiring process took too long is a great time to share the benefits of a phone screening followed by a panel interview. You may have to take the lead on how to set up the panel, create the scorecards, and develop consistent questions, but in the long run your hard work will pay off in successfully filling more job requisitions and placing candidates who succeed.

Next, you learned the importance of determining the purpose of an interview as well as the primary objectives. As technology continues to impact the recruiting profession, the only certainty you have is that you will continually change and improve the way you interview. Ask yourself if you're now putting a premium on the time you spend planning, obtaining relevant information from your hiring authorities, and understanding how your candidates will be evaluated *before* you begin to interview. Doing this will result in you presenting the best candidates.

We also addressed the importance of timing and how it has been impacted by technology. It's amazing how you're expected to find the best talent at warp speed. With people on both sides of the recruiting process, you've learned to effectively pre-close so you can align the time frame of your candidates with the time frame of your hiring authorities. When done right, timing will be your best friend, not your worst enemy. You've learned you can't control time, but you can control what you accomplish in the time you have, which is why you've learned to focus on the best use of your time.

You learned the importance of pre-closing, preparing, and debriefing both candidates and hiring authorities to eliminate surprises. Each time you are blindsided by an action of either your hiring authority or candidate, review your process to see when and where you missed information that could have prevented the situation.

You work too hard to have preventable issues result in rejection of offers. You've also learned how to extend offers that will be accepted without hesitation. An offer should be your reward well done, not put you into a sweat. If you've effectively pre-closed both parties, you should understand what offer will be extended and exactly what offer your candidate will accept. If you experience offers that are declined, implement the process outlined in Chapter 6 to all but eliminate the frustration of having offers rejected.

Chapter 7 is critical to your success, because so many recruiters drop the ball once they've placed someone in a job. This is where the high-touch factor is critical. Technology can help automate some of the follow-up process, but nothing has the impact of you personally reaching out. You are not only evaluated on the number of requisitions you fill, you are judged on whether the candidates you hired or placed become productive and retained.

Review Chapter 7 and implement the suggestion that resonated with you most, first. Imagine the benefit to you of all but eliminating no-starts, counteroffers accepted, and costly turnover. Too often, we dismiss these actions as the bad behavior of our candidates when there were actions you could have taken to prevent these issues. Remember, each time you point the finger at someone, there are three fingers pointing back at you. Continue to ask yourself "What could I have done different to prevent this from happening?" That will help fine-tune your skills throughout your career.

Also imagine the benefit of having 40 percent of the candidates you represent coming to you as the result of referrals. This can become your reality when you prove to your candidates that you care about them, can be trusted, and do what you promise. When you place or hire someone and don't keep in touch, they will feel you failed at all three, and you will not obtain referrals.

If you don't have a candidate referral program, this is a chance for you to step up by volunteering to spearhead this effort. When presenting your ideas, always discuss how everyone will benefit by having a structured, step-by-step referral program. Often referrals come from candidates you didn't hire or place, because they still want you to help them in the future.

You learned that the candidate experience is also critical to your success, which is why you need to provide resources to the candidate you don't hire or place, which can total as much as 95 percent of the candidates you attract. If you don't have a resource, I would suggest you review a sample of our career portal at www.myjobsearchresources. com. You could set up a customized career portal for your company in less than 10 minutes, and the perception is *you* created it. For more information contact my office at support@staffingandrecruiting.com or by calling 219-663-9609.

Chapter 8 is critical to your success, because it focuses on how important your role is in the high-tech, high-touch approach to recruiting. You will learn how to adapt a balanced approach while maintaining a positive attitude and daily motivation. This chapter addresses how to balance conflicting priorities, handle difficult hiring authorities and candidates, and how to overcome hiring authority objections and problem areas. Chapter 8 also explains how technology will continue to impact recruiting and the need for you to embrace change throughout your career.

Chapter 9 was written for third-party recruiters and explains how they can effectively sell their services to prospective clients. They don't have the luxury of in-house hiring authorities who must utilize their services. This chapter is critical for anyone pursuing a third-party recruiting profession, teaching you how to select your niche, identify the best prospects, overcome common client objections, differentiate from your competition, and how to write business you will successfully fill with top talent. You will also learn various pricing models and how to elevate your relationship from vendor to trusted advisor or consultant.

Lastly, I need to share a story with you about another mistake I made for years. Every time I read a great book, attended a conference, or watched training online, I would get very motivated and would try to change too much, too fast. We are all creatures of habit, and it takes 21 days of repetition for you to replace a current habit with a new one.

For that reason, I would strongly suggest that you pick only three things you learned from reading my book and implement one every 21 working days. Then review your results and implement your second idea. This will guarantee that the valuable time you've spent reading my book will provide you with a return on your investment of time and money. In addition, there is a website you can access with additional resources.

If you want to guarantee that you adopt new habits, identify an accountability partner. This could be someone you work with who has also read my book, or anyone else you know who is trying to elevate their success. Your accountability partner does not have to be someone in the talent acquisition or recruiting profession. It should, however, be someone who is also striving to excel in their profession.

You share the first idea you will implement for the next 21 days and call each other after the 21 days to discuss your results. The idea you select must be something that is quantifiable. It can't be "I'm going to improve my attitude" because that would be difficult to quantify.

You will be more likely to implement new ideas when you know someone is holding you accountable. When you get slammed with 20 new job requisitions and hiring deadlines, it's easy to fall back to your old habits. However, if you're focused on implementing only one change *and* have an accountability partner, it's much easier to make changes.

You are in the greatest profession at the best time in history, which is why I always recommend our profession to every talented person I meet. I welcome you to follow me on LinkedIn and would love to hear your success stories or answer any additional questions you may have for me. Please send your questions to support@staffingandrecruiting.com.

Your attitude, goals, and expectations will have a great impact on whether you embrace these new techniques or return to your comfort zone. There is a price to pay to attain your next level of success, but I guarantee it is well worth your effort. The only reason I write, train, and speak is so the people I reach will become more successful. If you embrace the high-tech, high-touch approach to recruiting, your hiring authorities, candidates, coworkers, and *you* will benefit.

GLOSSARY OF RECRUITING INDUSTRY TERMS

Alternative staffing

Includes all nontraditional flexible work other than direct (permanent) full-time employment, such as temporary workers, contractors, consultants, part-time workers, self-employed workers, and independent contractors.

Blended

Describes the majority of contract, staffing, and recruiting firms that provide a combination of direct, temp, and contract services for their clients and candidates.

Candidate

Refers to an individual who has the qualifications to potentially fill a job vacancy. Typically, it is someone who has been prequalified for a position and submitted to a client company. In the contracting segment of our profession, the candidate becomes the employee of the contract staffing firm after being placed.

Client company

Receives services from a contract, temp, or direct staffing firm.

COBRA (US only)

US legislation enacted in 1986 that requires employers with 20 or more employees to offer continuation of health care coverage in the event that an employee is terminated or experiences a qualifying life event.

Co-employment

Two or more legally separated employers share potential or actual employer responsibilities for a common employee(s).

Contingent staffing

Flexible supply of manpower to support core employees during periods of increased demand.

Contingent workers

Classification given to workers who have non-full-time, nontraditional work arrangements. Includes temporary workers, contractors, consultants, part-time workers, self-employed workers, and independent contractors.

Contractor

Employee of the contract staffing company who provides services to a client company under the day-to-day supervision of the client.

Contract and temporary employees

The differences between temporary and contract employees are:

1 Contract positions are usually higher level requiring more specialized skills, such as IT positions.

2 Pay and bill rates are higher for contract work.

3 Contract assignments are longer than temporary assignments.

Contract or temp firm

These firms are the employer of record. Most of these firms offer benefits. The candidate works for the contract or temporary firm but is sent to various clients for a predetermined time frame and hourly pay rate.

Contract or temp-to-hire conversion fee

Candidate begins as a contractor or temporary employee, and after a predetermined period of time they are transferred to the payroll records of the client.

Some firms do not charge a fee if a certain number of hours have been worked.

Some firms charge a conversion fee or processing cost when their temp or contractor is transferred from their payroll to the payroll of their client.

Others charge a full or partial placement fee when a contractor or temp is hired by the client.

Conversion fee agreement

A conversion fee agreement should be signed for every contract placement. The financial details often differ, and the written agreement specifies details and avoids legal proceedings. This agreement usually provides that a fee is due if a contract candidate is hired as an employee of a client company.

Core employees

Traditional employees who have the skills and experience needed to help their employer attain goals. They are often supported by flexible contingent workers.

Direct contingency firms

These firms place candidates in full-time positions. They are paid by the client company only if the candidate:

1 Accepts a job.

2 Reports for work.

3 Remains on the job past the guarantee period.

The average fee is currently 25–30 percent of annual salary.

Downsizing

Employers lay off full-time workers in order to lower fixed costs and become more competitive in worldwide economy.

Employee benefits

Some benefits are mandated by US laws such as Social Security, unemployment, and Workers' Compensation. Others are an indirect form of employee compensation in addition to salary, which can include health care, life insurance, retirement, and other perks. The American Health Care Reform Act will impact benefit requirements.

Employee leasing

The core employees of a business are transferred to the leading firm's payroll and benefits resources. The leasing firm provides payroll, accounting, personnel management, employee benefits, risk administration, and human resource functions. In addition, they often offer management consulting and expertise to the subscribing business.

ERISA (US only)

Refers to the Employee Retirement Income Security Act. A US federal law that governs pension and welfare employee benefit plans. These are complex and extensive US laws that govern and set guidelines for employee benefit programs.

US Federal Unemployment Tax Act (FUTA)

FUTA is the term used for the payroll tax every employer must pay under this act. This tax cannot be withheld from the employee's pay. It is solely the responsibility of the employer.

Flexible staffing

Flexible supply of manpower to support core employees during periods of increased demands. Same as contingent staffing.

Independent contractor

An independent contractor provides services to a company but is not an employee of that company. The company pays the independent contractor without withholding payroll taxes or paying the employer's share of payroll taxes. An independent contractor has the right to decide how the work will be done and may hire others to assist or do the work. Independent contractors also do not receive wages. The IRS and states hold independent contractors under intense scrutiny because of abuses costing billions of tax dollars.

Managed service provider (MSP)

Refers to an organization that manages a customer's computer systems and networks, which are located either on the customer's premises or at a third-party data center. MSPs offer a variety of service levels from just notifying the customer if problems occur to making all repairs. MSPs may also be a source for hardware and staff for its customers.

Margin

Refers to the dollar amount difference between the client company bill rate and the employee (contractor) pay rate (salary).

Markup

Refers to the percentage that the client company bill rate is greater than the employee (contractor) pay rate (salary).

Multiplier

Refers to the quotient of the client company bill rate divided by the employee (contractor) pay rate. If an hourly bill rate is $30.00 and the hourly pay rate is $20.00, the multiplier is 1.5.

Outsourcing

Client company staffs an entire department by the employees of a staffing company, on or off premise. See Vendor on premises.

Payrolling

Refers to situations where all or a portion of a client-customer's employees are on the payroll of a staffing firm but working at the client-customer's location.

Payroll taxes

Employers are appointed as agents of the government to withhold US federal, state, and local income tax from employee's wages. These obligations are severely regulated and carry heavy penalties if they are not done correctly.

Recruitment process outsourcing (RPO)

A form of business process outsourcing (BPO), where an employer outsources or transfers all or part of its recruitment activities to an external service provider. The Recruitment Process Outsourcing Association defines RPO as follows: "When a provider acts as a company's internal recruitment function for a portion of all of its jobs." RPO providers manage the entire recruiting and hiring process from job profiling through the onboarding of the new hire, including staff, technology, method, and reporting. A properly managed RPO will improve a company's time to hire, increase the quality of the candidate pool, provide verifiable metrics, reduce cost, and improve governmental compliance.

Retained search

These firms charge one-third of their fee up front, receive one-third after they submit a certain number of résumés and are paid the last one-third when the candidate is hired. If they do not fill the position, they keep the first two-thirds of the fee.

Sole source

Using one company/agency to fill all of your staffing needs. A sole-source supplier allows a client company to go to one recruiting firm for all its staffing needs, whether the employees are direct, contract, or contract to hire.

Staffing company

The employer of contract candidates, which handles all responsibilities associated with payroll and administrative duties.

State Unemployment Insurance (SUI)

Each US state imposes a payroll tax on the employer for unemployment benefits. The employer is entirely responsible for paying the tax; it cannot be deducted from the employee's pay.

Technical contracting

Contracting jobs such as engineers, programmer analysts, systems analysts, designers, technical writers, and other IT and engineering jobs.

Traditional employment

Term for direct employment.

Triangular employment

Relationship between contract candidate, contract staffing company, and the client company where the contract candidate is the employee of the contract staffing company but performs services for the client company.

Unemployment insurance

US government-sponsored protection to assist workers who have been laid off or quit their jobs through no fault of their own. This insurance represents a contribution on the part of an employer as a percentage of the employee's gross wages.

Vendor management system (VMS)

A provider that handles order distribution or candidate selection for an employer. The VMS works between the client and staffing and recruiting firms. This eliminates direct contact with hiring authorities for the staffing and recruiting firm, and if someone is hired, the VMS company is paid a percentage of the fee or margin (average 2–3 percent).

Many larger companies are utilizing VMSs, and as a result, some staffing and recruiting firms have gone into the VMS business. The typical VMS system includes contingent worker sourcing, billing applications, supplier profiling, order creation and distribution, candidate submissions, on- and off-boarding, time- and expense-keeping, and reporting.

Vendor on premises

Outsourcing arrangement where a full-time staffing coordinator administers the entire outsourcing process for the client: interviewing, testing, screening candidates, filling job orders and contracts, issuing payroll, and providing on-site management of the department.

W-2 versus 1099 MISC (US only)

At the end of the year, US employees receive either a Form W-2 or a Form 1099 MISC. An employee who receives a W-2 has all required payroll taxes withheld throughout the year. An independent contractor receives a 1099 and has no payroll taxes withheld.

Workers' Compensation (US only)

Businesses are required by US law to obtain Workers' Compensation insurance for their employees. The purpose of this insurance is to provide medical and other benefit coverage for employees who suffer a job-related injury or illness. Generally speaking, the contract staffing firm must maintain Workers' Compensation for their employees or coordinate coverage through a subscriber.

INDEX

Lightning Source UK Ltd.
Milton Keynes UK
UKHW020810230321
380788UK00002B/14